Love Affairs

LOVE AFFAIRS

The Therapeutic Guide to Sound Thinking and Smart Moves after Infidelity

Joel Block, PhD

Sex, Love, and Psychology
Judy Kuriansky, Series Editor

 PRAEGER™

An Imprint of ABC-CLIO, LLC
Santa Barbara, California • Denver, Colorado

Library of Congress Cataloging in Publication Control Number: 2017045940

ISBN: 978-1-4408-6154-3 (print)
      978-1-4408-6155-0 (ebook)

22 21 20 19 18   1 2 3 4 5

This book is also available as an eBook.

Praeger
An Imprint of ABC-CLIO, LLC

ABC-CLIO, LLC
130 Cremona Drive, P.O. Box 1911
Santa Barbara, California 93116-1911
www.abc-clio.com

This book is printed on acid-free paper ∞

Manufactured in the United States of America

CONTENTS

SERIES FOREWORD

I've heard so many complaints about infidelity over decades of giving advice on radio, TV, and in print. "My husband had an affair and I can't get it out of my mind. What can I do?" "My boyfriend slept with my best friend and I hate her. How can I get back at them?" "My husband said it was a one-night stand but I don't believe it and I'm so depressed. Help!"

Interestingly, similar questions have persisted across decades, but the questions have even expanded in number and content, as contemporary life gets more complex, escalating threats to commitment. Sound advice to so many betrayed love partners is therefore relevant and urgent. Thus, this book is highly needed and exceptionally useful. In these pages, Dr. Block covers the issues counselors and couples need to know about how to handle these issues. Rightfully, he calls them "extra-relationship" rather than "extra-marital," as couples are increasingly not married these days. Artfully, Dr. Block explores types of affairs, emphasizing how emotional and psychological motivations greatly impact understanding and repairing the breach in the relationship. His vast clinical experience deciphers desire, in order to help couples handle the fallout from the betrayal. Further, his including real cases examples help clarify how therapy can really help.

Since an ounce of prevention is worth a pound of cure, "affair-proofing" your relationship is wise. Too many betrayed partners throw in the towel. Dr. Block's wise advice—with which I heartily agree—is that you can rebuild that essential trust, recover and recommit, even to a better state. It may take work, but as he emphasizes, it's worth it.

Dr. Judy Kuriansky

ACKNOWLEDGMENTS

With all my thanks and affection to:

The men and women who trusted me with a highly personal segment of their lives. And to my family. All of life, including a writing project, is sweeter with love, and I have been blessed with abundance.

AUTHOR'S NOTE

The identities of the people described herein were protected by altering names and various other external characteristics; the essential psychological and social dynamics involved have been preserved. Any resemblance to real persons is strictly unintentional; any identification with particular persons is, I trust, impossible.

The terms "husband" and "wife," "him" and "her," "relationship" and "marriage," require clarification. Often the conventional "him" was used because it is awkward to say "him" or "her" each time I referred to an individual whose gender was inconsequential; so, too, the use of "wife," "husband," and "marriage" is not meant to exclude those people who were not formally married.

Further, "extra-relationship" is more typically used than "extramarital" since about 18 million men and women are cohabiting in 2016. This is up 29 percent since 2007, when 14 million adults were cohabiting, according to U.S. Census Bureau data. Indeed, it is my hope that the principles and discussion outlined here will prove helpful to any two people engaged in an ongoing relationship, married, or not.

INTRODUCTION

THE LOYALTY CHALLENGE

The headline in the *New York Times* (*NYT*) practically screamed a warning at those in an ongoing love relationship, *New Love: Short Shelf Life* (Lyubomirsky, 2012). As the article states, "In fairy tales, marriages last happily ever after. Science, however, tells us that wedded bliss has but a limited shelf life."

The *NYT* article reports that American and European researchers tracked 1,761 people who got married and stayed married over the course of fifteen years. The findings were clear: newlyweds enjoy a big happiness boost that lasts, on average, for just two years. Then the special joy wears off and they are back where they started, at least in terms of happiness. The findings have been confirmed by additional studies.

The research simply confirmed what many of us in longer lasting relationships have realized, monogamy is a challenge. We humans are very complex. We want change, but we dislike disruption; we like the new, but we cherish the old; we desire thrill and excitement, yet we also put a premium on security; ambiguity seems interesting, but too much of it provokes anxiety; we may seek familiarity, but when we find it we become bored. This ambivalence is present in (http://www.apa.org/topics/divorce) all aspects of our lives, but in affairs of the heart, it is more acute and potentially more consequential.

To fit our multifaceted emotional beings into the confines of the marital or cohabiting arrangement is not easy. As a means of attaining fulfillment for two individuals, the institution of marriage and other long-term romantic arrangements has limitations and imperfections.

THE DESIRE TO MERGE

Of those who are married, the divorce rate in our country is very high. According to the American Psychological Association, about 40 to 50 percent of married couples in the United States divorce. The divorce rate for subsequent marriages is even higher at 67 percent (Kreider & Ellis, 2011). Yet, marital or other long-term relationships offer something significant to many people, for the great majority of those who divorce remarry. Marriage and cohabitation is not disappearing.

Despite the discouraging statistics warning of the risk that comes with counting on growing old with a lover, the institutions are alive, if not thriving. Critical to these oft-chosen living arrangements for most people, the formality of marriage or cohabitation comes with a sense of harmony and the promise of fidelity, even if it is unspoken.

We commit to what we hope will be a lifelong relationship despite most of us knowing that even at its best these institutions cannot meet all the needs of both parties all the time. Our lives are not conducted in isolation; men and women are in contact with numerous other people every day, whether face-to-face or Facebook, text, Twitter, or phone. As a matter of course, they will experience satisfactions from these encounters. Some men and women are not only undisturbed that "outsiders" serve in this capacity but also relieved that they themselves are not obligated to meet each and every need or whim of their mates.

But what if that need or whim is sexual? Faithfulness being ordinarily seen as faithfulness in the flesh, sexual transgressions have always been highly disturbing. The momentousness of sex, though exaggerated by our culture, produces emotional turmoil. Temptation creates more of a conflict in the sexual area than in any other area of life simply because we value sex so highly today. Sex is high on the charts of all media, books, TV, movies, theater, and certainly in social media and the Internet generally.

MODERN TIMES AND THE COMPLICATIONS

Adding to the mix, attraction to people other than one's mate is also "in." Actually, it always has been—the mere fact that there are men and women establishes attraction as a constant. However, in years past when the average life span was between twenty-five and thirty-five years, and when married couples and their families lived and worked in small self-sufficient units, the opportunities for realizing one's desires for emotional/sexual involvement outside marriage were severely limited. Our ancestors were confined not only by stricter views of the obligations of wedlock but also by the technological restrictions of their time. Now, with urbanization, larger communities, greatly improved mobility, and especially social media, easy access to a slew of dating sites, and eased social restraints on sexual behavior, extra-relationship sex is not only more tempting but far more realizable.

While sex outside a committed relationship is more available, hence more tempting, it is not more acceptable. In fact, a *NYT* article (Friedman, 2015) citing a 2013 Gallup poll states, "Ninety-one percent of Americans find infidelity morally wrong; more than the number that reject polygamy, human cloning or suicide."

While we decry those who are untrue, the number of Americans who actually cheat on their partners is rather substantial: "Over the past two decades, the rate of infidelity has been pretty constant at around 21 percent for married men, and between 10 and 15 percent for married women, according to the National Opinion Research Centers Social Survey at the University of Chicago's independent research organization."

There are 9 million couples in live-together relationships—18 million people. The limited research that exists on committed but unmarried couples suggests infidelity in those relationships is also a factor. A study published by University of Denver researchers followed a nationally representative sample of 993 unmarried individuals in committed opposite-sex relationships to explore predictors of first-time infidelity. It found that 14 percent had "sexual relations" outside of the relationship over a twenty-month period, and 43 percent of those broke up after the infidelity (Shaw et al., 2013).

Those are the statistics of the extent of infidelity; they are not necessarily a big surprise, and they are probably understated since more than a few individuals are likely to be apprehensive about disclosing such sensitive information. The article continues and reports on an aspect of temptation that is less commonly known: "We are accustomed to thinking of sexual infidelity as a symptom of an unhappy relationship, a moral flaw or a sign of deteriorating social values . . . it turns out that genes, gene expression and hormones matter a lot."

NURTURE MEETS NATURE

As a psychologist specializing in couples and sex therapy, I have become increasingly sensitive to individual differences and understand that some people are more attracted to the extra-relationship experience. In fact, the *NYT* report cited previously (Friedman, 2015) highlights a less known factor in infidelity, a genetic predisposition to seek novelty and adventure, including affairs; it should not be considered startling. Our genes may be hardwired in some ways, like eye color, for instance, but in other ways, including the temptation to wander, choice is still on the table. It is just that the temptation may be naturally stronger for some than it is with others. We are a product of nature and nurture, and for all of us some issues and impulses are more difficult to master than others.

In a world so impersonal, so disconnected, so unconcerned about the individual's needs, and so filled with Internet temptations in the form of social media, dating sites, "life is short, step out" sites like Ashley Madison as well as loads of pornography, many of us find that a committed long-term relationship provides only part of what we hunger for. If that hunger turns to lust—the sexual and psychological excitement of a new person—the ground rules forbid us to go further than fantasy. But human nature is not rebuffed by the restriction; rules beg to be broken.

Affairs are, and always have been a factor that, at some level and at some time, those in relationships have on their "concern" radar. From the one-night stand to the grand amour, including emotional affairs that are not sexual and the vast popularity of Internet porn it is hard to escape the reminder of temptation from conversations with friends, as well as the ever-present media exposure.

Whether or not we approve of the incidence of extra-relationship liaisons, we cannot reasonably deny that this is a subject of considerable interest to nearly all adults; those who have been touched by the issue; those simply curious, and those in the helping professions whose offices often house the crisis of discovery. It is hoped that a book on extra-relationship sex that bridges the gap between imagination (the novel) and numbers (the statistical-based study) has a place on our book shelf. It is the goal of the author to offer evidence-based guidelines along with decades of clinical experience to those struggling with the painful dilemma of infidelity.

The content in the following pages is not intended as a prescription for or a proscription against infidelity. The purpose has not been to condemn or condone; it has been to produce an honest guide to the risks, consequences, and the positive aspects, as well as traumas, traps, and treatment suggestions for one of the more enticing complications of relationships, the affair.

As to "the affair," the definition also varies among people. Someone who has had a casual sexual encounter may not consider the behavior "stepping out," since to them it is thought of as meaningless—despite their partner viewing the experience quite differently. Others may consider all types of physical involvement an affair, not just intercourse. Still others, more likely the involved rather than the noninvolved partner, may not label the behavior a breach of trust, if there wasn't intercourse.

There is also the issue of emotional infidelity, and other behaviors—for example, an unconsummated Internet romance, a "happy ending" massage—that weakens or breaks a relationship's spoken or unspoken loyalty agreement as to what constitutes infidelity.

Further, within each general category of breach there are variations. For example, emotional infidelity could consist of an Internet relationship, a work relationship, or a long-distance phone relationship. Sexual infidelity could consist of visits with sex workers, phone sex, or same-sex encounters. Added to the complexity is the extent of the breach—was this a one-time behavior or a long-lasting experience? Is this the first time a breach occurred or a relationship replete with broken promises? Then there is the state of the relationship prior to the breach—is it a solid relationship that is likely to survive a breach or one that was teetering even before the breach?

How about the emotional state of the partners in the primary relationship? Some people are more sensitive to trust breaches, perhaps by history or temperament, others with more emotional resources may be able to handle a broken trust with somewhat less acrimony and suffering.

In the pages to follow while a particular example or discussion may only include a particular behavior, all of the above factors are considerations as well. Infidelity as is being discussed is referring to a breach of the expectation of sexual/emotional exclusivity.

Thus, as noted earlier, infidelity can comprise a number of labels and activities including "having an affair," "extramarital relationship," "cheating," "sexual intercourse," "oral sex," "kissing," "fondling," "emotional connections that are beyond friendships," "Internet relationships," "pornography use," and others (Blow & Hartnett, 2005). All serious breaches but varying in intensity and impact based on the view of the noninvolved partner.

All forms of "stepping out" are oft-times considered a severe transgression and violation to the commitment in a relationship and may evoke a myriad of feelings for both partners including, but not limited to, betrayal, disappointment, shame, guilt, and sadness (Fife et al., 2008a; Hall & Fincham, 2005). Additionally, both emotional and sexual infidelity are significantly associated with relationship dissolution (Negash et al., 2013) and can have deleterious implications on the family (Nemeth et al., 2012).

In essence, what constitutes an act of infidelity depends on the type of relationship that exists between people and the agreements, spoken or unspoken, between them. Indeed, even within an open relationship where partners see others for sexual liaisons, there are rules to be followed to protect the stability of the primary relationship. When those rules are broken, the stability of the relationship is as subject to threat as conventional relationships.

Chapter 1

DESIRE AND PREVALENCE

We live in a world that is challenging for relationships. The eight-hour workday for many people is a thing of the past. The workday is frequently longer, often the commute adds substantially to the day, and social media temptations on the Internet beckon to us, stealing even more of our time. One thing is certain: while the development of an enduring relationship provides a degree of emotional fulfillment not afforded by other options in life, it is also more demanding and fraught with more perils and temptations on busy, fully engaged lives than most of us realize.

When a lover gives a committed partner everything a mate doesn't—compliments, attention, gifts, and love notes, along with that most important and seductive factor, time and attention—it becomes a challenge to resist. When the primary relationship has been neglected, partners feel bored, unfulfilled, neglected, and pressured by their overscheduled lives. The thrill of being with someone new, whether it is an office romance or an Internet flirtation, makes a person feel sexy and alive; it can be a powerful lure.

Once an affair has occurred, it usually serves to erode intimacy further. Intimacy requires honesty, openness, and self-disclosure. The deception that accompanies an affair makes this impossible. In addition, if the affair partner becomes the confidante for problems in the primary relationship, it can be even more threatening to that relationship because it creates a bond of friendship between the affair partners that goes beyond sexuality. Shared secrets tend to bind people, while they create distance from those who are excluded.

There is also the all-important affection factor and mutually satisfying love-making. The DINS (Double Income No Sex) relationship is more common as couples struggle to meet their expenses. The problem of low-or-no-sex marriages is coming out of the closet. A flurry of recent books, TV coverage, and watercooler talk are drawing new attention to the matter. Research by Denise Donnelly (1993) of Georgia State University, reported in *The Journal of Sex Research*, found that 16 percent of couples fail to have sex at least once a month, a pattern that predicted marital unhappiness and divorce.

Some may assume it is women who are at the heart of the no-sex phenomenon. Wrong! Women aren't the only ones refusing sex. In her research of married people in sexually inactive marriages, Dr. Donnelly found that in 60 percent of the cases, it was the man who had stopped the sex. The reasons for low or lack of sex in marriage vary, from extra-relationship affairs to poor conflict management, child care, fatigue, and job stress. All this to say that despite the busy lives we lead and the impact it has on primary relationships, ironically both men and women seem to find time for secret liaisons.

A SAMPLING

Heather, a forty-six-year-old medical social worker who had never before been separated from her live-in partner of sixteen years, was seated at a professional convention next to Marty, a physician in his early forties. They got to talking; she found him immensely charming and intelligent, and eventually their contact turned sexual. Halfway through the night, they became lovers. She spent three carefree, flirtatious days with him; then the convention ended, and they went their separate ways to homes only sixty miles apart.

Heather, for her part, reacted to the experience rather dramatically: "My outlook on life was completely changed. The affair made me aware of my frustrated need to think and to communicate with someone I felt tuned in to. Before, I had been living with a sense of incompleteness without knowing it. It was a painful realization; and one that led me to end my relationship. Yet I do not regret what happened. I would rather be aware—know what I want and not have it—than to live out my life without ever having known. But it's been difficult. There was a time when I looked forward to my future with Marty; it was a comforting, secure thought, growing old together. Now those images are agonizing. He has been hurt."

The experience also had an impact on Marty, though a substantially lesser one. "Heather was the first real affair I had since I got married. I felt guilty about the affair, and as a result, I lavished more affection on my wife, Jill. I was restless and dissatisfied with my marriage, but I had no desire to get out of it. Several women at the hospital were becoming increasingly attractive to me; secretly I was hungering for a woman to grab me and seduce me. I'm not a passive man, but I felt so obligated to Jill that I thought it would be necessary for another woman to be very aggressive. That was all fantasy. When I met Heather, I practically accosted her. I didn't let up until we made love. The last night of the convention we spent together was the closest I had felt to anybody in a decade."

Heather and Marty maintained contact over the next year. He would occasionally ask her to spend time with him; sometimes a few days, sometimes just an afternoon. She was now separated and he was still married. In between visits, she went out with other men. Although they grew closer and considered themselves in love, neither spoke of an exclusive commitment. Heather was convinced, instead, that fairly soon their affair was going to end. The way she saw it, she had two choices. One was to find someone else who was available for commitment; the other was to continue in the present relationship as long as it lasted. She was leaning toward the latter.

Heather spoke of her arrangement in a quite firm voice:

"I couldn't get myself to ask Marty to leave his wife for my sake. He'd been pressured all his adult life by his wife; I wouldn't allow myself to become an additional pressure. Besides, it would backfire. His wife had driven him out with her nagging; he started staying away from home taking on more and more work, to avoid her whining and I was determined not to be categorized with her.

"Anyway, his wife wasn't my competition; she was a non-person to me. Marty went places without her whenever he could. She didn't care, so long as she was given enough money for her expensive tastes. A couple of times a week he spends the night at his office where there is an attached apartment, he tells his wife he has too much to do to come home. That's where I go to be with him; he prefers not to stay over at my house. With my children nearly grown, I feel able to move into his place for a couple of days at a time, but usually he becomes restless and finds some way to suggest it's time for him to get back home. He says it's for appearance's sake, but I don't believe that; it's because he wants to be alone—he isn't the kind of person that wants to be around anyone for any length of time."

****

George is a fairly typical banker, specializing in real estate, who comfortably maintains a suburban country club lifestyle. He was born and raised in an upper-middle-class WASP (white Anglo-Saxon Protestant) family and married an almost ideal WASP woman with whom he has lived contentedly for the past nine years. They have three well-adjusted children. He is not really unhappy about the life he leads; he is quite satisfied with his present income, and he makes a point of not joining in the heavy drinking and womanizing at banking conventions.

On occasion, George travels to nearby cities for several days at a time in connection with his work. He accepts these trips as part of his responsibility but certainly does not regard them as the highlight of his job. One such trip that he had anticipated with some apprehension turned out to be much more productive than he had imagined. At the conclusion of the day's business, he arranged to finish up the next day, one day earlier than expected. He was pleasantly surprised and quite relieved. On the way out, he met his business contact's secretary, Muriel, and was struck by her appearance; she was small and slender, almost childlike, with black shiny hair in an Afro. Her face was long and her eyes, though surrounded by excessive makeup, were bright. She was, at most, in her late twenties.

"Just before I left the office, I did something impulsive and very odd for me. I asked Muriel out to dinner. Surprised and a bit apprehensive, she accepted. At dinner, I found her to be a hell of a good conversationalist—quick, incisive, and unafraid to express her opinions. When she spoke, she looked even prettier. There was something about her warmth and personality that attracted me. It was as if I were a very impressive person. After dinner, I dropped her off at her apartment but I couldn't get her out of my thoughts. In the morning, I felt a definite excitement as I called to arrange the next day's business and the next evening's dinner with Muriel. I questioned this: 'I'm a married man, I'm happy, what the hell I am doing?' But all I could think of was being with Muriel.

"It was crazy, I felt like a teenager again. I learned that there were a number of men in her life, but I didn't care. She was good company and I enjoyed talking with her; that was enough. But was it? Back home thoughts of her kept intruding while I was at the bank or in the house playing with the children. I found myself looking forward to rather than dreading my trips to that city. In her company, I felt light, playful, something I'd never really experienced before. I was brought up to be staid, emotionless, and compulsively achievement-oriented. Muriel was easygoing; she had a devil-may-care attitude that was infectious. One evening, she kissed me good night. Up to this point, there had been nothing more than innocent hand holding crossing a street. I wasn't really ready for more. Just breaking my usual 100 percent business and efficiency routine was monumental for me. The thought of getting involved was overwhelming."

After he had known Muriel for about eight months, George began to have a change of heart. The lack of sexual intimacy started to bother him. It was like an unfinished project. Not that things were bad at home. He was having regular and satisfactory sexual relations; there was a mutual warm interchange between himself and his wife. Nor did he find Muriel all that attractive. Yet, the longer he continued to see her, and the more they spoke and texted on their phones, the more he became obsessed with making his move. On the one hand, he feared that an overt, bold approach might offend her, but on the other hand, he felt compelled to break the brother-sister pattern.

"I was considering all this when one stormy February night Muriel turned to me and suggested we take a suite at the Plaza. With a mixture of relief, eagerness, and anxiety, I agreed immediately. That first night, we made it, if that's what it's called. I wasn't really that excited, so I wasn't able to maintain a full erection. As usual, Muriel was very warm and understanding. We wrote it off to the awkwardness of the first time. But the sexual thing never really improved. On other occasions, I felt passion in stops and starts, but I was never really able to maintain the excitement long enough until I started using one of those erection drugs. That gave me the boost I needed, but I learned something: extra-relationship liaisons are too much of a strain on me. Although my wife didn't notice a change, I did. I have been preoccupied, ill at ease—probably feeling guilty. I've decided: no more."

****

The names we give the experiences just described are extra-relationship relations, stepping out, infidelity, adultery, unfaithfulness, affairs, and cheating. Women and men, men and women, the attraction between the sexes, the basic desire of the one for the other, is often not limited to the marital/relationship partner. The human condition implies a continuous search for love and attention, sometimes diverted but other times aggressively sought and passionately set into motion. The extra-relationship sexual involvement is a tempting source of diversity and fulfillment; it is a major issue on the minds of millions of people who claim to be committed.

Most of us take the same attitude toward extra-relationship sex that we take toward paying our income tax. As Morton Hunt contends in an early book on the subject, *The Affair* (1971), "Many of us cheat, some more, some less; most of us who don't would like to but are afraid; neither the actual nor the potential cheaters among us are prone to disclose the truth or defend their views except to a few confidants; and practically all of us teach our children the accepted moral code, though we neither conform to it ourselves nor expect our children to when they have grown up."

Whatever our convictions about infidelity, our fascination with it is endless, as evidenced by the popularity of the subject in movies, novels, and drama. The portrayals are sexy and dramatic, and while they often don't end well, the real-life drama may be less dramatic, but is often as painful. Infidelity typically causes severe relationship instability, precipitates a loss of trust, and increases conflict, undermining a couple's sense of togetherness and shared identity (Agnew et al., 1998; Glass, 2002). Extra-relationship affairs often result in separation and divorce (Weeks & Treat, 2001). In addition to the harmful effects on the relationship, infidelity can have serious individual consequences. The betrayed partner may experience a torrent of emotional struggles including depression, rage, feelings of abandonment, rejection, lowered self-esteem, and loss of confidence, as well as symptoms of post-traumatic stress disorder (Cano et al., 2000). Unfaithful partners may also experience emotional struggles related to the events that have transpired, such as guilt, anger, embarrassment, and loneliness as well as depression.

MEN AND WOMEN: NOW AND THEN, HERE AND THERE

To be or not to be monogamous is for most coupled people in today's Western culture a perplexing decision, and the choice is becoming more difficult in more relationships all the time. Infidelity is on the increase. The late Dr. Alfred C. Kinsey's (1948, 1953) statistics, based largely on interviews conducted nearly seventy years ago, revealed a remarkably high incidence. Since then, encouraged by the birth control pill and by an atmosphere of growing permissiveness concerning all sexuality and the increased opportunities the Internet affords as well as more women being in the workplace, sexual roaming has increased considerably. The prevalence of the institution of marriage and other committed living arrangements is matched only by the prevalence of the transgressions against it.

Through the ages, and in most cultures and societies today, there have been rules for the maintenance of the marriage system and proscriptions against breaking the rules. Yet as Pamela Druckerman suggests in *Lust in Translation: Infidelity from Tokyo to Tennessee* (2007) that the grass has been greener on the other side, "regardless of where the turf is located—Africa, Europe, Asia, or America, in cold climates or in warm ones, among the white, black, and yellow races." As Dr. Druckerman notes, there are extra-relationship connections in every country and on all continents. Adultery persists in the face of powerful taboos and the most stringent religious dogmas. Human desire has never been confined to the institution that narrows it, even though that institution has endured and prospered.

Despite the limitations set upon extra-relationship sexual relations by practically all known cultures, the definitions of the term and the means of enforcing conformity vary widely among societies. The outstanding issue in most preliterate and ancient societies was not sexual morality, even though many of us today interpret it so. Primarily adultery was considered a threat to the economic stability of a society and specifically to male property rights. Wives were property and the privileges of property owners superseded the desires of chattel. Additionally, men wanted to be sure of the genetic heritage of their heirs. The ancient Hebrews, for example, were less concerned with the Seventh Commandment in a moral sense than with the necessity that a man knows who his son was so he could retain economic and social power over him. Thus they severely punished adulterers, because they put a son's paternity in doubt.

Indeed, the behavior pattern designated as "marriage" would probably never have been invented if groups of men had not feared the mate-stealing of their fellow men. This concept of mate as property is readily observable among primates, the mammals most closely related to humans. The males treat mates they have acquired as property to be defended against the aggressions of other males, yet both males and females have an apparent propensity to take advantage of sexual opportunities with others. With regard to men in more current times, sociologist Dr. Robert N. Whitehurst's study "Extramarital Sex: Alienation or Extension of Normal Behavior" (1969) concluded it is often inevitable; he notes:

> Given certain average conditions in the married life of the males involved, it is possible to predict an adulterous outcome for a great number of males between the ages of forty and forty-five that may be created out of natural conditions arising over years of marriage. . . . Recent research shows that marriages, contrary to the togetherness notions extant in our culture, do not, through time, become characterized by increasing depth and intensiveness of communication. Instead, there is some evidence that time takes its toll in regard to the importance of the relationship.

While historical, anthropological, and sociological data fail to reveal a society that has consistently suppressed and severely punished its males for extra-relationship relations, for females the cultural situations have been quite different. The majority of human societies that have been studied by social scientists completely prohibit and severely punish sexual relations by a married woman with anyone other than her husband. It is a rare society that freely permits women extra-relationship sexual relations; more usually, they are permitted under special circumstances.

In an occasional society, it is the custom for a male to lend his wife to his guest. In other situations, sex is permitted, or even required, between a wife and her brother-in-law, for example, during certain religious celebrations or as part of the marriage ceremony. Yet even in these relatively rare societies with rather lenient attitudes toward female extra-relationship sex, such activity is tolerated only because it is not seen as a threat to the security or masculinity of husbands; after all, it is carried out under their rules and with their control.

But times have been steadily changing, if not so much in societal restrictions, then in women's adherence to these restrictions. There has been a significant change, for example, in the incidence of extra-relationship sexual experience among American women: they are having sexual relationships outside their marriages by an earlier age than did women in Kinsey's time. This change has been highlighted on the cover of *Newsweek* magazine (Ali & Miller, 2004) with the headline, *The New Infidelity: From Office Affairs to Internet Hookups, More Wives Are Cheating Too.* As the authors of the article, Lorraine Ali and Lisa Miller, state, "With the workplace and the Internet, overscheduled lives and inattentive husbands—it is no wonder more American women are looking for comfort in the arms of another man."

The double standard implies that boys will be boys, but girls are supposed to behave properly. Not anymore. Much has changed since Emma Bovary chose suicide with arsenic over living her life branded an adulteress—humiliated, impoverished, and stripped of her romantic ideals and dignity.

Today, *Sex and the City*, movies like *Unfaithful,* and a myriad of magazine articles and novels have made every imaginable sex act fodder for cocktail party conversation. Women who are adulterers are no longer tragic figures to be scorned or stoned. They are more likely living next door, quietly, conventionally, at least on the surface.

When Carmela on the HBO series *The Sopranos* took a lover after putting up with Tony's antics over the years, audiences gave her a standing ovation. And it is not that affairs are a media event without a big following in reality. In *Newsweek*'s cover story on this made-for-Hollywood issue, they report that couple therapists estimate the number of women who have had sex outside their marriage is close to 40 percent, compared with 50 percent of men, and the gap is almost certainly closing.

Are these startling figures accurate? Hard to say because when people talk about sex in studies of various sorts, from the less formal to the rigorously controlled, results vary wildly. Men, not surprisingly, tend to amplify their sexual experience, while women tend to minimize it.

Despite the possible unreliability of the numbers, the trend is clear. With more women in the workforce—nearly 60 percent of women work outside the home—temptation and opportunity are more likely to collide. That has certainly been the trend I have witnessed over nearly three decades working with couples.

We can see the building incidence of women getting extra-relationship involved in increasing numbers from Kinsey's time to current times. Two reliable and largescale studies of American sexual behavior demonstrate the increase. While Kinsey's research was done in the 1940s, a new round of studies that was published in the 1970s shows the trend. A study of 2,372 married women was conducted by Robert R. Bell and Dorothyann Peltz; the results were published in *Medical Aspects of Human Sexuality.* The other, a study of some 1,500 married men and women, was conducted by the Playboy

Foundation and published as a book, *Sexual Behavior in the 1970s*, with a text by Morton Hunt (1974).

In Kinsey's day, it was only by the age of forty that a little over a quarter of the women surveyed had had extra-relationship experience. Bell and Peltz found that the extra-relationship experience had been had by the same percentage of the women they surveyed by the age of thirty-five; they predicted that when all members of the group they had chosen to investigate reached forty, 40 percent of them would have had extra-relationship experience. The Playboy Foundation's statistics were even more startling. Its figures showed that while in Kinsey's time only 8 percent of young wives—those under age twenty-four—had reported an extra-relationship sexual experience, by 1972, 24 percent did. Conclusion: Extra-relationship sex among women is rapidly approaching the male pattern. Indeed, if the numbers are accurate in the *Newsweek* article previously cited, the jump has been startling and steadily rising.

One thing is certain: while the development of an enduring relationship provides a degree of emotional fulfillment not afforded by other options in life, it is also more demanding and fraught with more perils and temptations on busy, fully engaged lives than most of us realize. When a lover gives a woman everything her husband doesn't—compliments, jewelry, flowers, and love notes—along with that most important and seductive factor, his time and attention, it becomes difficult to resist.

Not to be left out, men, too, feel bored, unfulfilled, neglected, and pressured by their overscheduled lives. The thrill of being with someone new, whether it is an office romance or an Internet flirtation that makes him feel sexy and alive, can be a powerful lure, and often it is.

Once an affair has occurred, it only serves to erode intimacy further. Intimacy requires honesty, openness, and self-disclosure. The deception that accompanies an affair makes this impossible. In addition, if the affair partner becomes the confidante for problems in the primary relationship, it can be even more threatening to the primary relationship because it creates a bond of friendship between the affair partners that goes beyond sexuality.

Of course, when asked, if they would consider an affair, would a woman acknowledge that temptation? Perhaps not, but again we see the trend rising. In 1991, the National Opinion Research Center at the University of Chicago asked women if they'd ever have sex outside their marriage, and 10 percent said yes. When the same pollsters asked the same question in 2002, the "yes" responses rose to 15 percent, while the numbers for men stayed flat.

COMMITTED RELATIONSHIPS: A PARADOX

Despite the cultural restrictions against extra-relationship sex on the part of wives and the quasi-intolerance of the sexual affairs of husbands, the evidence is overwhelming that a great deal of adultery occurs. No relationship today is felt to be immune:

Marjorie: You mean Al's never been off with another woman?

Dolores: Not as far as I know. Why should he? He seems happy.

Marjorie: Why should he? Why should my Martin, why should any of them?

Dolores: Al just doesn't seem interested in other women.

Marjorie: How old is he?

Dolores: Thirty-nine.

Marjorie: Men, it's part of their personality. He'll be starting any day now!

Marjorie's prediction may be bold and unsettling, but it is too broad in its prediction for all men. Research is not definitive, but it is closer to accurate than Marjorie's broad sweep. There are a number of studies that investigated personality aspects of infidelity. Prominently among them is the use of the Five-Factor Model of personality (FFM), a set of five broad trait dimensions or domains, often referred to as the "Big Five": *Extraversion, Agreeableness, Conscientiousness, Neuroticism* (sometimes named by its polar opposite, Emotional Stability), and *Openness to Experience.*

A key question raised in the research was would the personality of married couples predict marital infidelity? A meta-analysis of forty-five studies examined personality factors underlying sexual risk behavior and found high agreeableness and high conscientiousness reliably correlated with lower sexual risk taking. In contrast, infidelity is significantly associated with low agreeableness and low conscientiousness. The researchers (Schmit, 2004) also found that those with high levels of agreeableness and conscientiousness were higher in relationship exclusively, which suggests they are less likely to be unfaithful.

Then there is the gender factor. In addition to personality factors, gender is often cited as making a difference. It has been found in various studies that men do appear to be more likely to have affairs than are women (Glass & Wright, 1992; Allen et al., 2008); however, this difference is largest among older couples; in younger couples, women may be as likely to become affair-involved as men (Atkins, Baucom, & Jacobsen, 2001; Atkins et al., 2005). Women also seem to be more prone to emotional infidelity—falling in love or forming an emotional attachment outside of marriage—than to purely sexual infidelity (Blow & Hartnett, 2005), and not all research takes this into account. For example, researchers may define an affair specifically by sexual intercourse with someone other than a primary partner (e.g., Allen et al., 2008; Whisman & Snyder, 2007), which complicates capturing the frequency of emotional infidelity, which is more likely to be initiated by women.

It is at least a possibility that, with emotion-based affairs included, the gender difference in frequency may be considerably smaller than currently is accepted. Other individual factors related to higher rates of primary relationship infidelity include higher incomes (Blow & Hartnett, 2005; Atkins, Baucom, & Jacobson, 2001), marrying relatively young (Atkins, Baucom, & Jacobson, 2001), and more previous sexual experience (Whisman & Snyder, 2007). In contrast, strong religious belief has been associated with lower likelihoods of infidelity in some research (Atkins, Baucom, & Jacobsen, 2001).

If we don't fall into one of these categories, personality or otherwise—age, income, marrying younger, and so forth—does that suggest that the rest of us are not vulnerable? Not quite. It may be speculated that nearly everyone feels the temptation to wander sexually during married life or any long-term love relationship, whether very occasionally and only in fantasy, or often and in the flesh. Longer life spans, greater leisure, and freedom from many of the medical and economic ills that once preoccupied us have encouraged us to raise the level of our emotional aspirations. We expect a lot more than our ancestors did from marriage—heightened sexual passion, continuous love, emotional security, stimulating companionship, and thorough compatibility.

Since childhood society has impressed upon us the promise that marriage will bring total physical, emotional, and social fulfillment. For many, though, particularly those who believed the romanticized notions of what marriage would do for them, the disappointment comes quickly, passion cools, and interest wanes. The fire is banked, and as time goes by, fewer and fewer sparks are struck. The excitement of discovery, of having novel emotions and impressions, of conflict, of finding new ways of sharing, becomes more and more infrequent as mates come to know each other more fully. The marriage may become boring, stale, and empty.

For some, this kind of belle indifference comes amazingly soon, as noted by the research in the *New York Times* article cited previously. For others, it's postponed for years. Evidence indicates, however, that eventually it comes to the great majority of marriages and other long-term relationships in some degree. One major research study involving hundreds of families showed that the longer people lived together, the less satisfied with the arrangement they became. This generalization held up even for marriages that were thirty and more years old (De Paulo, 2015).

"Monotony," "the treadmill," and "humdrum" are words that describe states of feeling from which most of us usually want to escape. This seems true whether tedium stems from eight hours on an assembly line, from eating the same food day after day, or from going through the same old motions with the same person, saying and thinking and doing similar things, endlessly. "Satiation" is the technical word for it. "Fed up" is somewhat more blunt. This is the human condition, and it is not necessarily an indication of neuroticism or immaturity. In fact, this is due to adaption—our innate ability to get used to things, good or bad. We are pre-programmed to adapt, and if we had not evolved toward adapting as a species we would have long been extinct.

Consequently, even those of us whose committed relationships are satisfactory may not be fully protected from fantasies of infidelity. With the passage of time, this becomes increasingly true. The face that excited, the touch that electrified, the personality that stimulated, eventually become merely comfortable, like the living-room sofa. Most of us can tolerate this for a time—we absorb ourselves in work, an avocation, and our children—but as the years pass, we may experience a mantra, "Is this all there is? Am I to die without ever falling in love again?" This may include the woman, now nearing forty, whose private anguish is growing older and seeing her beauty fade. And the not–so-youthful, slightly paunchy man sitting next to a lovely woman on the commuter special from Connecticut can't help but wonder, "With her, could I recapture it all again?"

We all want to live the complete life: to have the security of a long-term relationship like marriage and the variety and excitement of the single life. This is difficult to do when extra-relationship sex is involved because the issue calls into play a fundamental human paradox: A person feels most fully alive when he or she can be stimulated by the challenge of the unknown and yet have the security of the known to give him the confidence he needs to try something different. The pleasure of being alive depends to a considerable degree on the ability to include both known and unknown elements in one's life, but if an extra-relationship—emotional or sexual relationship—is chosen as the medium, particularly the main medium, for providing newness and excitement, the likelihood is that it will threaten the security that is a prerequisite for its appreciation.

The solutions to the commitment dilemma are varied. Some people find lovers despite the risks; others experiment with group marriage; others work at finding contentment within their relationship and suppress their extra-relationship desires; still others don't, they divorce.

Psychologists, sociologists, and others confronted by the marital dilemma have suggested numerous dramatic and imaginative if not always practical alternatives to traditional marriage; this was especially the case during the 1960s and 1970s also known as a time of sexual liberation. The social movement of the time challenged traditional codes of behavior related to sexuality and interpersonal relationships throughout the Western world from the 1960s to the 1980s. Sexual liberation included increased acceptance of sex outside of traditional heterosexual, monogamous relationships (primarily marriage). The normalization of contraception and the pill, public nudity, pornography, premarital sex, homosexuality and alternative forms of sexuality, and the legalization of abortion all followed.

During this period, Robert Rimmer (1966), a writer of utopian novels, notably *The Harrad Experiment*, suggested that two couples with their children join together in a corporate marriage, pooling all their resources—sexual, emotional, and economic in a kind of double-the-pleasure togetherness. In the novel, at Harrad College, where controversial coed living situations are established, the students are forced to confront their sexuality in ways that society previously shunned. Also, during the period of sexual questioning, some advisers suggested compulsory birth control and stiff prerequisites for obtaining a marriage license. Other social scientists promoted open sexual agreements for all couples; others deplored this solution as neurotic and self-defeating. Even "term" contracts in marriage, lasting anywhere from five to twenty years with options for renewal, had been proposed.

Proponents of "permitted" adultery, more often referred to as "open marriage" tend to be particularly dogmatic in their insistence that extra-relationship sex helps make "closed relationships" more permanent and enjoyable. They argue that many, if not most, divorces are caused by the desire for sexual experimentation, and that permitting sexual variety within marriage will therefore forestall or eliminate divorce. Traditionally, marriage has been defined as an arrangement that promises both permanence and exclusivity. The proponents of open sex hope to attain greater permanence than is customary these days by letting the exclusivity go.

But would sexual experimentation within marriage necessarily eliminate divorce? Judy's opening remarks during her first couple therapy session are pertinent here: "We agreed to have occasional affairs provided we kept them light. My husband feels betrayed by me. His affairs had indeed been casual, but mine had become involved. He felt my love for him had become weakened or else this wouldn't have happened. It is my goal in couples therapy to get back together but he's growing very distant. He wants a divorce and, of course, I blame myself. I see that for me, affairs are dangerous because they so quickly get out of perspective."

Judy's experience turned out to be far from being a panacea; sexual sharing is also a threat to security because many people find it difficult or impossible to keep to the ground rules. On the other hand, some authorities, blinded to the fact that some are not only capable of functioning with extra-relationship allowances but seem to thrive on them, rigidly insist that this behavior is always inimical to marriage and should be fought against and squelched.

Avoid the heartache of an affair by loosening the boundaries of sex within a relationship? The research on open marriage or "swingers" is mostly absent or poorly done as to the longer-term results, compared to traditional relationships. Social groups considered to be on the fringes of acceptable sexual behaviors (swinging, open marriages, group marriages, polyamory, and communes) have been largely ignored by the research community. The justification given for the lack of research is the difficulty in getting research funding for these topics, little academic reward or recognition for researchers, and the assumption that a fear of AIDS has restricted, or eliminated, these behaviors (Moors & Schechinger, 2014).

Anecdotally, it appears there are those it works for: "My husband and I do swap partners. We have enjoyed it very much overall. We have traveled as far as 4 states away to swap partners. It is real fun and it keeps your sex life alive. My husband loves our next door neighbor's wife. He takes her trash out each week just to spend an hour or so with her each week while her husband spends some nights in my arms."

In contrast, another experience: "While swapping partners may sound like a good idea, please be careful. What if you fall in love with another swinger? Hopefully your marriage is made up of a lot more than sex. My wife and I tried that a couple of times fairly early in our marriage, but one of us felt uneasy with it so we stopped. Stopping was not a bad idea because some of those in the 'Lifestyle' end up involved with someone else and their marriage crashes. As a male, I was enthused at first, but I had to admit, it was a danger to our marriage."

Obviously, any given solution will enhance the primary relationship of some couples and prove destructive to that of others. The advocacy of a single specific lifestyle is useless: what may apply to one person will not apply to another; and what is true for one person at a particular moment in life may not be true for that same person at a later moment. Over the centuries, we have been offered numerous formulas by self-proclaimed saviors, revolutionaries, prophets, behavioral scientists, and philosophers, and not one of them has proved ideal for all. Ideal solutions exist only in an ideal world; in the real world, the best we can do is seek options that fit our individual natures and do not violate our cherished values. In this society, and with our emotional equipment, group marriage or open sexual sharing produces jealousy and conflict for most of us. Though these solutions work for some people, they hardly help the majority who live in a conventional marriage contend with the tensions and anxieties of adultery.

CAN YOU SEE IT COMING?

The German philosopher, Schopenhauer, told the story of two porcupines huddled together on a cold winter's night. The temperature dropped; the animals moved closer together. But then there was a problem: each kept getting "stuck" by the other's quills. Finally, with much shifting and shuffling in changing positions, they managed to work out an equilibrium whereby each got maximum warmth with a minimum of painful pricking from the other. Many husbands and wives have something in common with the huddling porcupines. They want to achieve and maintain a kind of equilibrium; warmth and closeness, but without the sometimes agonizing "pricking" that comes from continuous interaction with another human being.

This brings us to a key question: does current research support the prediction of infidelity? Can a man or woman in a primary relationship tell if his or her partner is prone to infidelity? As noted earlier, there are personality factors and some demographic data that are associated with the inclination to be unfaithful, but that data are far from fully predictive. Nonetheless, the idea of being able to predict a strong proneness to infidelity is enticing.

Several researchers have looked at this factor closely in an attempt to take the prediction possibility further. For example, Weis and Jurich (1985) found that people who are well educated, who are from large metropolitan areas, who have permissive attitudes about premarital sex, and who are dissatisfied with their marital relationship are more accepting of infidelity. In their analysis, those who frequently attended church were also more likely to disapprove of adultery. However, other researchers expressed caution about their results based on the statistical analysis they used (Blow & Hartnett, 2005).

There are issues of opportunity, and other variables, like culture; type of primary relationship; the behaviors that make up the infidelity to take into consideration, for example, oral sex, kissing, sexual intercourse, history of love connections, and prior experience with infidelity. Another group of researchers (Olson et al., 2002) also found that risk factors include gender, with men being more likely to have affairs, and race, with African Americans being most at risk. Age is also a factor, with younger couples more at risk. Other risk factors include employment status, with those working outside the home being more at risk, infrequent church attendance, and low marital satisfaction (Liu, 2000; Treas & Giesen, 2000). As for low marital satisfaction, although most couples report high marital satisfaction, the odds of having an affair increase 28 percent when a person reports that he or she is "very" happy in the marriage as opposed to "extremely happy" (Treas & Giesen, 2000).

Apparently there are a lot of variables, and it appears that the research to determine a formula that alerts couples to infidelity is not there. Too many contradictions exist, some research findings conflict with others or come up with findings that other groups do not, or the focus is on one group—age or otherwise—that does not apply to other groups.

To get closer to an answer, at least as a general consideration, here is what a team of researchers (Allen et al., 2008) concluded in their search for predictive factors: good communication lowers the probability of a host of marital issues, including infidelity. They state, "Just like the famous 5:1 ratio of positives to negatives associated with greater marital success over time (Gottman, 1994a,b; Notarius & Markman, 1993), our findings suggest that positives need to far outweigh negatives. For example, couples without infidelity evidenced an average of an approximate 4:1 ratio of validating to invalidating behaviors, whereas couples who went on to experience male or female infidelity evidenced a ratio of around 2.4:1."

As in most aspects of life, there are few guarantees, but it appears that more positive interaction in comparison to less negative interaction—particularly, validation, the kind of communication that boosts the feeling of acceptance—provides a definite edge. In fact, data presented by Atkins et al. (2001) suggest that individual factors such as religiosity may only be protective in the context of a good relationship system. Thus, it is beneficial and perhaps even protective against infidelity for all couples to work on maintaining positive and supportive communication with one another.

Positive versus negative communication is a powerful factor early on as well. From a premarital perspective, researchers also found the type of communication between relationship partners to be an important predictive factor. Premarital self-report and observational data were compared for couples who experienced infidelity and those who did not experience infidelity in the first years of marriage. Couples in which the male engaged in marital infidelity were characterized, premaritally, by significantly lower male sexual satisfaction, lower male positive communication, and higher female invalidation, whereas couples in which the female went on to engage in infidelity were characterized, premaritally, by significantly lower levels of female positive communication, higher levels of male and female negative communication, and higher levels of male and female invalidation (Allen et al., 2008).

Returning to the two porcupine's analogy, adultery as a means to "smooth the rub" is a high-risk undertaking, particularly for a person who is fairly happy in general and relatively satisfied with his or her relationship. Probably only a small percentage of men and women in our society have fully freed themselves of deep-seated anxieties and guilt about extra-relationship sex relations, and still fewer have mates who are similarly free. If the unfaithful partner is free of anxiety and guilt, he or she may still be concerned about being dishonest with a mate who would disapprove if the truth were known. And even where reciprocal knowledge and approval exist, frequent or extended extra-relationship sexual activities can produce negative effects on marital and personal happiness by draining time, energy, money, affection, and other resources from the primary relationship.

Some men and women enter into an affair confident that there is very little chance of being found out. As one man wrote: "I was guided by the conviction that we had it all figured out, that the reward was worth the risk, that the secret wouldn't be revealed, that my heart was meant to be followed."

He was wrong, and in this instance following his heart led to destabilizing his family. Feelings about the outside relationship cannot help but affect behavior within the relationship. The signals may be ever so slight and subtle such as an inability to concentrate, a fleeting and mysterious smile as thoughts of the lover flit through the mind, periods of inattentiveness to the spouse followed by unusually fierce demonstrations of affection, being preoccupied, distracted, all coming with excuses, but the perceptive partner will notice these new behaviors and in time begin to wonder.

As one woman expressed it: "He just started acting differently. Nothing I could really put my finger on, but it bothered me and then suddenly the thought jumped into my mind, 'He's having an affair!' When I asked him about it, he told me the truth and my whole life came crashing down around me. I thought we had so much going for us and then I came to this hideous realization that the person I thought I was married to wasn't the person I was really married to at all."

Immediate feelings of pain and anger usually result in the stipulation that the straying mate either end the outside involvement or leave; occasionally, a husband or wife will attempt to adjust to the partner's affair. "She's a good wife and mother, all in all," one man said. "And maybe I haven't the right to insist she stop seeing the guy she is sleeping with, since it doesn't seem to affect our relationship all that much." But in a later conversation with this same man, he confessed that, "It just can't work. I go to the office every day and I sit there wondering whether she's with him. I imagine them in bed together. It's torture."

Nor do the problems end here. Suppose this man's wife had not been discovered but found herself sexually charged by the affair. What does she do with her drive? How does she cope with the powerful feelings that dominate her but cannot be shared with her husband? If she tries to share them, how can she help comparing one man to another, and if her husband is found wanting, what does she do with her feelings? Bury them and bury her newly kindled sexual responsiveness, too? Or, respecting her right to those feelings, does she embark on a succession of affairs? Or does she divorce her husband? And if she is secretive about her indiscretions how does she explain the restlessness, the missing hours in her week, and the staring into space her husband asks her about. Those are just some of the complications for her; the emotional complications for her husband will likely overwhelm those of his wife.

Probably what underlies the most severe anxieties concerning our mate's extra-relationship sex is a fear that we are losing control: control of our spouse, control of the relationship, control of the future, control of ourselves. This fear of loss of control rooted in insecurity is quite common today. As we lose control of other sectors of our lives (or discover we never really had control), we wish all the more to be secure in our intimate relationships and our family life. If things are unstable elsewhere, at work, in our country generally, the stability of the home becomes all the more important.

This fear of the loss of our partner's emotional bond, of the love, affection, and support he or she provides, can be terrifying. It is to insure ourselves against these anxieties that we consent to ethical proscriptions of extra-relationship sex. When we suspect our mates of transgressing this agreement, we become anxious and defensive. We assume that if we lose our mate, it will be to someone else; consequently, we begin to view others with suspicion. Such behavior makes us less attractive, it promotes aloofness and tension in our marital partner, and, as in a self-fulfilling prophecy, we become more suspicious and our basic fear of loss deepens.

An example may illustrate the problem more clearly. In couples therapy, one frequently sees both spouses engaging in behavior they consider the most appropriate reaction to some wrong the other is doing. For instance, a wife may have the impression that her husband is not open enough for her to know where she stands with him, what is going on in his head, what he is doing when he is away from home, and so on. Quite naturally, she will therefore attempt to make herself more secure by asking him questions, watching his behavior, checking his phone, and tracking him in a variety of other ways. He is likely to consider her behavior intrusive and react by withholding from her information that in and by itself would be quite harmless and irrelevant—"just to teach her that I am not a child in need of checking."

Rather than making her back down, her husband's reaction increases her insecurity and provides further fuel for her worries and her distrust: "If he does not even talk to me about these little things, he must be hiding something." The less information he gives her, the more persistently will she seek it, and the more she seeks it, the less he will give her. It is not long before the drama evolves to a point that Dr. Paul Watzlawick (1974) and his associates describe in their book, *Change*, as reminiscent of two sailors hanging out of either side of a sailboat in order to steady it: the more the one leans overboard, the more the other has to hang out to compensate for the instability created by the other's attempts at stabilizing the boat, while the boat itself would be quite steady if not for the insecurities of its passengers. It is predictable that unless something changes in this situation, the occupants of the (marriage) boat will be under constant unnecessary strain or, worse yet, finish up in the water.

There is very little doubt that extra-relationship sexual relations complicate a committed relationship. Does this mean that the adulterers are then bad or evil? Certainly not bad or evil, but adultery involves breaking a promise and lying, and it is one of the most serious promises we make. Partners have made a promise to have an exclusive relationship with one another, which includes abstaining from having sex with other people and in most cases avoiding an intense emotional relationship with a potential partner clandestinely. When this promise is broken, it is painful and indicates indifference on the part of the offending partner, even if that indifference is likely to be disputed if the offending partner's infidelity is discovered. Denial aside, it is likely to be assumed that he or she doesn't care that the other partner's feelings and well-being are at stake.

As we've seen, the evidence from in-depth studies shows that although in many circumstances an extra-relationship affair severely damages a relationship and family, there are other circumstances, albeit a minority, where it is of small consequence; and in still other circumstances, again a distinct minority, where it may awaken an individual to his or her emotional needs and capabilities or cause the end of an unsatisfactory relationship and allow both partners to pursue healthier options.

Those who choose to remain faithful are confronted with drawbacks as well as rewards. Some, even though unsatisfactorily married, forgo both infidelity and divorce because of severe self-doubt, or for religious, social, or ethical reasons. Their penalty is some degree of frustration and unhappiness. Yet there are rewards: their choice leaves them secure and easy in conscience. Others, though suffering equally from unmet desires and dissatisfactions, sublimate these desires, redirecting them into compulsive work, homemaking, or similar activities. This choice also has its reward: a productive output that is more socially and personally acceptable than illicit sex and love.

Some people work hard at their relationship and are fortunate enough to achieve a happy, satisfying union. They have few unmet needs and remain faithful with little effort. Even the desire for "something new" is relatively weak and passes or is directed back toward their mates without great difficulty. On the other side, a glance at the statistics, as we have seen, points to a large and growing number of people who have decided to take the chance and defy the monogamous code.

Discussing this informally with many psychologist colleagues who treat couples revealed that they initially felt that each individual should weigh his or her decision to have an affair or not according to the motivating circumstance, the kind of extra-relationship engaged in, and the effects on all concerned. Asked, if it is to maintain the current primary relationship with "supplementation"— or, is it an exit maneuver, prompted further thought. After additional discussion several of this small group (of seven psychologists) amended their response and suggested couples therapy as a first consideration, emphasizing that an affair is a breach of trust under just about any circumstance, and especially distressing if discovered. They felt a relationship that continued to be unsatisfactory even after competent-led couples therapy may be a candidate for mediated separation. While difficult, the consensus was that it is the more ethical choice.

In essence, it remains the responsibility of each of us to take into account our own needs, those of our mate and children, and the probable effects of our acts on all connected with us. The choice is not up to society—or even to psychologists that treat couples; it is each person's decision to make.

The purpose of this book is to help with the journey. It is intended for those people touched or troubled by, or just plain curious about, extra-relationship behaviors that violate relationship trust, including married, living together couples. In addition, it is for those therapists who are facing distressed couples in the consulting room. The author has treated nearly a hundred affair-involved couples over a long career, and the intention is to assist the reader to take this difficult journey with a guide.

Sound Thinking and Smart Moves

1. Trust is at the heart of a love relationship. Without trust relating is superficial and is a mere parody of intimacy. While temptation often surrounds us, in the workplace, on the Internet, and places in between, it is important to bear in mind that at least one person is likely to be seriously hurt in a violation of trust.

2. There are few guarantees in life, including being free of some form of infidelity, either as the involved—even if only struggling with the temptation—or suffering a broken heart as a result of a breach of trust. An intimate relationship, where feelings can be voiced without judgment and are validated, is likely to lower the probability of an affair. While agreement is optional in a relationship, feeling understood is not. Without being understood, there is no real relating.

3. You are having coffee or lunch with an attractive colleague or friend of the opposite sex. If you are looking for a guideline as to how to conduct yourself, consider imagining your love partner listening to the exchange. If your love partner would be put off, perhaps your exchange is crossing a line.

Chapter 2

TYPES OF AFFAIRS

TYPE MATTERS

Affairs, like other types of relationships, vary. Blogs and forums throw around the word "affair" as if they are all equivalent. In some manner they are—violations of trust—but depending who is on the deceived end of a breach, and that person's emotional sensitivity, there may be a world of difference. For example, for some people putting a workplace emotional connection in the same context as a year-long, deeply emotional, sexual relationship is like making an equivalent comparison between rolling a Stop sign and driving impaired with alcohol. Others may be more shaken by the emotional connection than "just sex." Properly identifying the type of affair that has occurred or is occurring is important because it has implications for an intervention and may guide the betrayed partner toward a decision regarding the future of the relationship.

Views on types of affairs are offered by the formerly affair-involved on blogs like "After the Affair Advice" and academic researchers like Douglas LaBier, PhD. Here, a sampling from the blog, by a former self-confessed cheater (https://affairadvice.wordpress.com):

> The *Double Life Affair*—This type of infidelity occurs when the affair-involved cheater has very little emotional attachment to his/her spouse and the affair is all-encompassing. The *Emotional/Non-Physical Affair*—The lack of sexual involvement is often used as a rationalization as to why it's not an affair. The *Opportunistic/One-Night Stand Affair*—Frank Pittman in his book, *Private Lies*, (1989) calls this "the Accidental Affair." This type of affair is usually unplanned and is usually due to

an impulsive decision in which the "accidental" lovers were lost in the moment. It's not unusual for alcohol to be involved in the liaison. The *Exit Strategy Affair*—As indicated by the name, in this type of affair the partner who strays is unhappy in the relationship and stepping out is meant to signify the end of the relationship. The blog mentions a few more—the *Serial Cheater/Sex Addict Affair*, the *"I'll-Show-You"/Revenge Affair*, and the *Love Is My Drug Affair*.

With some overlap, Dr. LaBier suggests that his study of affairs led him to six types, including the *"It's-Only-Lust" Affair*. La Bier states that the "about sex" affair is most common. According to him, it can feel really intense, but it's also the quickest to flame out. The *"I'll-Show-You" Affair*. This is the revenge affair borne of anger and resentment toward a partner after years of an unhappy relationship. The *"Just-in-the-Head" Affair*. This is the emotional affair, intense, but no sex involved. The *"All in the Family" Affair*. This affair encompasses a full romantic/sexual involvement with a family member, like, for example, an in-law. The *"It's-Not-Really-an-Affair"* affair occurs when the available partner believes that the other really will leave his or her partner, given enough time and patience and rationalizes, "It is true love and not an affair!" The *Mind-Body Affair* is the one that Dr. LaBier considers the most dangerous one of all for the lovers' existing relationships. He notes, "It's so powerful because it feels so complete, emotionally, sexually, intellectually, spiritually."

As noted, affairs are almost as varied as relationships, which vary extensively. Despite the varied nature of affairs, much of the research on infidelity still use extra-relationship sex, usually interpreted as intercourse, as the target variable to be studied. That omits a variety of affairs that do not include intercourse. Consequently, some researchers are shedding light on infidelity by asking participants about "affairs" and leaving the extent of involvement open to interpretation. That makes sense in light of the fact that a growing literature demonstrates that individuals do consider a broader range of involvement, including sexualized Internet relationships, to constitute "infidelity" (e.g., Whittey & Quigley, 2008).

One group of studies on infidelity emphasizes a range of types of infidelity including one-night stands, emotional connections, long-term relationships and philandering, cheating, sexual intercourse, oral sex, kissing, fondling, friendships, Internet relationships, and pornography use (Blow & Hartnett, 2005). However, most of the literature divides infidelity into less-broad, more-specific categories including sexual infidelity, emotional infidelity, combined sexual and emotional infidelity, and Internet infidelity (Glass & Wright, 1985; 1992).

Moreover, within each general category there are different subgroups. For example, emotional infidelity could consist of a workplace relationship or a long-distance phone relationship. Sexual infidelity could consist of visiting sex workers, same-sex encounters, and different types of sexual activities. There is also another type of infidelity: online infidelity, a process whereby individuals involved in a long-term committed relationship seek computer contact with an opposite sex member. Further, men and women view types of infidelity differently. Women take a stricter view of what is considered infidelity (Oberle et al., 2016).

In consideration of the type of involvement, whether it is on the Internet or in the bedroom, there is one overriding factor—the extent of the involvement. It can range in involvement from flirtation to life-changing. Moreover, just as an extra-relationship involvement ranges in the degree of involvement, so do romantic relationships. Some couples have relationships that are more habit and familiarity than intimacy. Other couples have been able to maintain a high level of emotional involvement through the course of their relationship. The type of primary relationship, emotionally intense or closer to superficial, and the type of affair matters. That is, the type of extra-relationship involvement combined with the involvement in the love relationship is an important determinant for how they will impact each other and is the present subject under consideration. Hence, the following involvements to ponder.

LIGHT 'N' HEAVY

"When I travel or go to an out-of-town business meeting, it is my custom to seek out a woman to share my bed. It's novel, it's exciting. An hour, a day, or a week later, I say good-bye and return to my family. Sometimes I think of a lover for a week or two after the encounter. We may even work it out to meet again from time to time. But although I am flirtatious, playful, and I come on pretty aggressively, I think it is also apparent that I am distant. No e-mails, no texting, and phone contact is also out. I don't want someone contacting me and me forgetting to delete the contact. I never let myself fall in love with any of the women, nor do I think any of them have ever really fallen for me. This is deliberate. Aside from the fact that my primary commitment is to my wife, I am very busy. I couldn't handle any more than an occasional fling. There are even times when I'm away from home and too busy to fit it in. Of course, if I could have a woman delivered to my room, I wouldn't turn it down, and there are occasions when I haven't. But to go searching and go through the wining and dining thing, sometimes I just can't be bothered. With me, the issue is unencumbered sex, rubbing up against new flesh. If it gets burdensome, forget it. I have enough of that already."

* * * *

"Sex to me isn't just a roll in the hay. It's very important. When I first met Barry seven years ago and he came on to me with his sexual liberation line and 'let's get it together' and all that, I quickly straightened him out. He felt rejected and pretty insulted. My reaction was he got what his hand called for! Over the next year or so we continued to run into each other with our respective spouses at social gatherings. Then my husband suggested we invite Barry and his wife to dinner. I went along with this and we began to see more of them. I had this vague feeling of discomfort back then when this was occurring. What happened to me was that I was falling for this guy. Knowing me, this spelled trouble because when I fall, I really plunge. And that's what has happened. Barry and I have been linked romantically for five years now. I see him on the average of three or four times a week. We still get together socially with our mates, although not as often as several years ago. Neither Barry nor I encourage it. It's not a comfortable scene. Even after all these years and tons of rationalizations, being in that situation still feels fraudulent. My hope is that one day we will each untie our present marital knots and live together openly as husband and wife."

****

It is apparent from these two descriptions that to leave out the intensity of an affair of any type would be a serious omission, perhaps most important of all is the intensity of an affair. Infidelity ranges from the occasional one-night stand to the once-in-a-lifetime grand amour. The types of affairs men and women choose vary in their implications and consequences both for the person and the relationship. Indeed, for an activity admitting of such diversity it would be possible to draw up a systematic matrix including many combinations of duration, seriousness, and intensity, and discuss each category separately. Although this would be a thorough approach, it would be unnecessarily complicated, for stripped to their basics, types of affairs, regardless of the type of interaction, come down to this: those of relatively low emotional involvement and those of higher emotional involvement. These are the two broad categories discussed in this chapter.

NEVER BECOME SERIOUS

Generally, in low-involvement affairs, meetings are sporadic, or if frequent, scarcely add to or deepen the secretive relationship. Of least significance here is the kind of relationship that takes the form of coquetry. This includes the normal flirting and minor conquests that are part of every social gathering. Conceivably, more serious in its implications for the primary relationship is the one-night stand, sex as play, a sometime thing that usually leaves little residue except perhaps residual guilt. More regular meetings may take the form the French label *la matinée*. This is a playful relationship between working men and women who use the lunch hour or afterwork "relaxation period" for their rendezvous. The basic rule for such a relationship is "Never become serious." The hazards include being found out, and that one partner might fall in love and thus become serious.

Casual sexual experiences may occur in relationships described as good as well as in those termed "bad" or "difficult." The individuals may be liberal or conservative, straitlaced or perennial "chaser" types, and rich or poor. Although sometimes the product of a meticulous plan, these affairs are often spontaneous pairings of the moment. They may be highly pleasurable or the reality may fall far short of fantasy. As the adulterous heroine of Erica Jong's classic *Fear of Flying* asks in a moment of satiric bitterness, "Why is it all so complicated? Why do you have to risk your whole life for one measly zipless fuck?"

The fantasy may be tantalizing but all sorts of things can go wrong: the pairing may be poor (a partner may prove inconsiderate or inadequate); illicit sex, counter to our society's mythology, may be discovered to be an inhibition rather than an aphrodisiac; guilt and anxiety may enter the drama; the motel, apartment, or whatever may turn out to be seedy, unsuitable, distasteful, and so on. In general, though, even when a brief extra-relationship encounter has not been altogether pleasurable, some people feel pleased with themselves for having had the experience.

Randolph, a forty-seven-year-old psychologist, looks placid, content, and uncomplicated. His features are sharp and clean. His hair is graying, giving him a distinctive appearance, and he dresses well but conservatively. His tastes and many of his convictions stem from a conservative base. Over the past several years, his conservatism has been slowly dissolving. In fact, he is rather proud of his departures from orthodoxy. Raised in a comfortable Irish Catholic suburb, he became an agnostic during his college days. This was perhaps his most difficult and profound life change because religion had played a major role in his childhood. Forsaking beliefs that to some extent had guided his life called for a dramatic psychic reorganization. Characteristically, Randolph had worked at restructuring his "life rules" in a cautious, deliberate manner. It was many years before he felt as comfortable with himself as he did when his religious beliefs were strong.

Randolph attended Harvard for eight consecutive years until attaining his doctorate in experimental psychology. He was more thing-oriented in those days, designing elaborate apparatus and complex animal experiments were his forte. He rejected working with people in psychotherapy because psychotherapists were "soft-headed" scientists who dealt with intangibles. This, too, changed over the years as Randolph took further training, and he eventually became a clinical psychologist. It was during his last year at Harvard that Randolph met his wife Jean, then an editor of a popular weekly magazine in the Boston area. Her attraction for Randolph was immediate. After two years of dating regularly, they married. Soon after they were married, Randolph was drafted and shipped overseas. Though he was away from her for months at a time, he never went prowling in search of another woman; in fact, he even had a difficult time envisioning the unfaithful act. In the early years of his marriage, if confronted at a party by a tempting body, he refused to let go and speculate on what it would be like to test that unknown flesh. After several years of marriage, when Jean took their daughter for a six-week summer visit to her folks in Austria, desire tormented him in the night and he consciously decided on an affair.

"When I decided to try finding someone I went out to bars where there was a friendly atmosphere and I'd meet all sorts of women. I was getting a lot of attention and I loved it. I was shy and inhibited in my teens and throughout most of my life. Until I met Jean at Harvard and fell in love with her, I had had no real romance. Now I was going out and I was really excited—and scared, very scared. One Sunday night I met a waitress who was very pretty, very warm, and very sexy. She must have been forty-five, but she looked much younger. She was married but separated for the past five months. She was also horny as hell but I didn't know that at first. She was a real lady, pleasant and proper. She seemed to enjoy my company without having anything else in mind.

"Overcoming my reserve, I asked her to dinner. She accepted. It was nice but I couldn't make my move! I asked her out again for the next night, and this time, although I wasn't sure what she had in mind for later, I knew what I had in mind. After dinner we went to my place and in a short time we were in a passionate position on the couch and decided to move into the bedroom. Once we undressed, things didn't go too well. I was so uptight I couldn't maintain my erection. Damn it, it was just as I've told my patients, 'The harder you try the softer it gets.' The irony of it all! All I could think of was, 'Doctor, heal thyself' but it wasn't easy. I know it must have been terrifically frustrating for her also, but she understood. Maybe she was used to it, who knows? In any case, I wasn't about to get into any long conversations about it. She wanted to stay overnight but, partially out of awkwardness and embarrassment about striking out sexually, I insisted on taking her home.

"The next day she called me and suggested we spend the evening together. When she said that, I got a sudden pang of anxiety but I decided to go ahead with it and arranged to see her. This time we got it on sexually. After meeting a few more times, though, another problem developed: I found it almost impossible to talk to her. Carrying on an extended conversation was actually painful. My interests were over her head, while hers were boring to me. Plus, and probably more important, I didn't want to put the effort into a heavy conversation. So, since we couldn't stay in bed all the time, we began to feel ill at ease with each other. After a couple of weeks of having seen each other for a total of six or seven evenings, our 'relationship' was over. It died a natural death. I think both of us knew from the start that this was a passing thing. There was never any talk of 'What do I mean to you?' or 'What are we going to do about all this?' or any of that commitment jazz. There was no entanglement. For me, that was fine. It was mostly the physical part that mattered to me. The interplay of personalities would have been nice had she been more compatible, but truthfully, it's just as well. The last thing I'd want is a real involvement. But I learned something: without some sort of involvement, the effort may not be worth it. It's a paradox; I don't need, nor do I really think it's wise, to get involved, yet a relationship based on nothing but sex is too limited. Granted, this time it was pretty good but that's because it was such a novel experience. Looking to the future, I really don't see myself doing this sort of thing.

"There's one wild aspect to this experience that really unnerved me. I wrote Jean a couple of notes during the time of my brief affair. One night she called and just as the conversation was ending, she said, 'Oh, by the way, dear, your Freudian slip is showing.' She refused to explain that. She just giggled. When she returned home in August I questioned her about that odd remark and she showed me the note I had written to her. The last line read, 'Wish you were her.' I was almost floored! After a forced laugh, I changed the subject. There was no way I was going to touch that!"

The lack of emotional involvement in Randolph's affair is not atypical. Occasional affairs such as these are probably the most common. When half the men and a quarter of the women in the Kinsey studies acknowledged that they had had at least one overt extra-relationship affair, most of them were referring to the shorter, lighter affair. In many instances, one or both lovers take deliberate steps to keep the affair limited. The strategies vary and include dating several people simultaneously so as not to lean on one too heavily; breaking off as soon as feelings get out of hand; setting limiting ground rules; deliberately alienating a lover who is pushing unwanted intimacy; and cutting down on meetings when emotional vulnerability becomes an issue. Of course, the away-from-home travel affair has many of these safeguards built in and is a favorite with those seeking low involvement. The primary purpose of these strategies is to keep one's real life private; by not disclosing themselves, the lovers seek to avoid intimacy and vulnerability.

Sometimes, though, people who avoid emotional intimacy in casual affairs are manifesting a more general style of relating. These people are usually uninvolved in their marriages also. Again, the strategies vary. Men commonly escape not only in affairs but in work and sports; women, in addition to pursuing affairs, may take shelter in household responsibilities, work, hobbies, and similar activities.

Frequently, the occasional affair is a kind of palliative for an aching relationship; it eases the pain without curing anything. That is just what some people want. They may lack the emotional apparatus for an intimate relationship. They remain in their primary relationship mainly for security and companionship, or because a committed relationship offers an established social role, a home base, children, and the rewards of being part of a family. When a relationship such as this breaks up, it is usually not because the occasional affairs stunted intimacy, which was lacking all along; it is more likely one mate wanted the intimacy and warmth the other did not provide. If both partners do not miss or need high involvement, the pattern of casual affairs may go on for many years without disrupting the marriage.

If a casual affair is not likely to have much effect on an uninvolved relationship, what does it do to an intimate marriage? This is very difficult to determine because the effects are varied and complex. For one thing, a loving, satisfying, and close relationship, does not preclude extra-relationship sexual involvement, it decreases its likelihood. One plausible generalization though is that an outside involvement will cause much greater strain in an intimate marriage than in a low-involvement marriage.

Diane, a heavy blond woman who is visibly graying, appears to be in her early forties. She has been married eighteen years and describes a period of her life when she had two casual affairs.

"Although these sexual experiences were meaningful to me, they were far from dramatic. I did not experience a grand awakening and I wasn't particularly enamored of my sexual partners. Yet I was excited and there was a change in me that I thought I was concealing successfully. I wasn't. One Sunday morning my husband turned to me in bed and said, 'I know people change as they grow, but when you live with a woman for such a long time, you get to know her very well; you relate to me in a certain way. In the past few months, a change has come over you. I don't know what to make of it. I don't know what's wrong, but you don't seem to be with me in the same way. Did I do something to provoke this?'"

Of course this kind of repercussion does not routinely occur in an intimate relationship. Some affairs may go undiscovered and even add to the individual and to the relationship. Nonetheless, the adulterous party takes a greater risk in an involved relationship. If the outside intimacy is emotionally intense as well as sexual, there will probably be subtle changes in personality and these are more likely to be detected in an intimate marriage. Typically, at this juncture, the adulterous mate will begin to lie: "Oh, it's my business troubles," or "I'm just edgy, I need a rest." If his mate does not buy these shaded answers, and suspicion continues to be aroused, the relationship is likely to create a growing distance and will probably deteriorate.

THE GRAND AMOUR

In my experience, the majority of men and women who believed their affairs were of minor consequence to their primary relationship described their affairs as shallow and short-lived or enduring but emotionally limited. Moreover, most of these people seemed to have primary relationships that were also emotionally limited. Responses were less positive and more flavored with conflict when their relationship was characterized by high involvement. When the affair was described as highly involved, that is, the lovers were sexually, emotionally, and intellectually attuned, their reflections on the experience were usually emotionally charged and filled with conflict.

Celia, a lively, attractive nurse with a slim but voluptuous figure, has been married to Joseph for twelve years. They have two children aged nine and four. Joseph is a successful, soft-spoken attorney who, in contrast to Celia's rather brash, agitated manner, gives the impression of sincerity and of being a take-life-as-it-comes sort of guy. Celia agrees with this description and adds:

"Joseph is solid and stable but he lacks something important. There is a certain excitement missing. He is predictable, practical, and proper. That's Joseph. There is no mystery; that certain impishness, growth potential, adventurousness is lacking. It's hard to pin down, but whatever it is, Justin has it. He's complex; you're never sure what he's going to do next. There's intensity and mystery. His eyes look out, but they also look in."

Celia met Justin three years ago in a therapy group just after she had her youngest child. Their mutual love did not come suddenly and irresistibly; it grew slowly as each of them became aware of the attraction and voluntarily continued an association bound to evolve into an affair. After eighteen months, Celia's love for Justin was all-encompassing, a synthesis of romantic passion and motherly tenderness. This was a love that grew not by absence and imagination but by nearness, merging, and sharing of experiences. At first, both Justin and Celia tried to suppress the enormity of their attraction for each other by reassuring themselves that what they felt was physical desire or mere infatuation.

This didn't hold up. The evidence of their feelings and actions was too strong for them to continue seeing their affair as merely a type of friendship supplemental to their primary relationships, but to admit that this was a potentially exclusive relationship would be acknowledging that their relationships were indeed endangered. There would be heightened disruption and instability in their lives until the conflict between the affair and primary relationship was resolved. Unlike the casual affair, which may coexist with a committed relationship, the high involvement affair competes with it directly. Celia continues:

"Justin and I phoned each other constantly. We saw each other three or four times a week. We were always on each other's minds. I became like an army commander, always prepared for every contingency. I knew exactly which restaurants to avoid because they were too big, noisy, and popular, and which to avoid because they were too small, quiet, and compromising. I became an expert on where to get my hair cut, washed, and set in record time and where to buy children's clothes without spending hours rummaging through stacks of mis-sized items. I had friends who could cover for me on days the housekeeper was sick; friends to help account for the sudden presence in my drawer of an expensive gift from Justin ('let's say you gave me this brooch. No, not gave. Why would you have given it to me? There isn't any special occasion. Let's say you know someone who is in the wholesale jewelry business and you got it for me at a third of its real price.'); friends who would tell me about movies they had seen down to the minutest details so that my reports to Joseph would be beyond question.

"Everyone in our circle except, of course, Joseph knew about Justin. No one approved, but no one would ever say a word to Joseph. They too knew him as a nice fellow, a sincere guy. None of them wanted to hurt him; to be the bearer of cruel tidings. Besides, people rationalized that things would be okay and that our marriage would survive. Justin and I weren't that optimistic. We realized that our relationships might be wrecked in the process. I suppose we both had our private thoughts about that—the guilt of breaking up a family; sizing up the emotional and security factors involved; considering money matters. I live comfortably, and realistically I know I wouldn't be happy to skimp and watch myself. We were, at base, scared. These thoughts were always present for me and for Justin also, although frequently they deferred to the passion of the moment.

"I recall an incident that occurred about a year ago. Justin and I managed to get away for a week in Puerto Rico. It was marvelous. Knowing that Justin had this thing about using every minute efficiently, I didn't interfere with his elaborate and detailed planning and went along with him on all the activities he chose. One day was a disaster, though. I wanted to go on a tour with him and he had other plans for us; I insisted, and he became more and more upset. He literally ended up in bed under the covers. When we talked it over later, he said that what bothered him so much was that he took our conflict as an indication that we could never live together harmoniously. He was so shaken by that projection that he felt ill. This is what I mean by a fear that loomed in the back of our minds—'will it work; will it last; am I risking my marriage only to lose everything?'

"Just as our affair was disruptive, it was also constructive and rewarding. Justin and I would make love and then lie side by side and talk for two or three hours and then make love again. We discussed the books we were reading, movies we had seen, the shape the country was in, my hopes and work aspirations, his work. We talked about our childhoods, our parents, our friends, our children. Each of us came to know almost everything the other was thinking and doing every day. We were childlike and we were serious, silly and intense, we were everything. When we were together the world stood still. Time stopped. It escalated and escalated until it was so emotionally intense, intellectually stimulating, and sexually arousing that it became the best thing each of us had ever known."

The conventional notion of highly emotional affairs is that such relationships follow a cycle: intense infatuation with a new person, a relatively quick decline in passion, disillusionment, dissolution, infatuation with a new partner, and a repetition of the cycle. Certainly some affairs fit this model, particularly since enormous emotional resources are required to lead two lives. As one woman, involved in a close relationship of two years, put it:

"I broke it off with Roger because I had built up a lot of resentment toward him over the two years. Conducting the affair had been more taxing for me than for him. I have children, lots of home responsibilities. He was on a much looser schedule. He was filling up free time with me, whereas I was sandwiching him into a very crowded life. It was restrictive. I never wanted to go on vacations, because I was afraid to be out of contact with Roger. I was always slipping away to make long-distance phone calls, or texts that I immediately deleted. My life was filled with subterfuge and it was no longer any fun. I couldn't relax; I couldn't get any rest. I had to make a choice, and since Roger would not make a firm commitment ('I don't think I could adjust to your children; let's just try weekends at first'), I chose my marriage."

This brings up another point. One reason high-involvement affairs are not that common is more practical than psychological: despite texting, emailing, and phoning, it is simply too difficult for most committed people to steal away for more than a few hours a week. Plus, there is only some time that a person can delete texts and clean their phone before it gets noticed. So although there may be a large number of people who dream of a grand amour, they simply cannot find the time to realize one. But this is not the whole story. In some prolonged, highly involved relationships, the cycle of infatuation, heightened emotion, decline, and dissolution follows a path similar to how it is in a good number of longer-term committed relationships.

These relationships, like many longer-term relationships, sometimes move from vitality and a strong erotic attachment to a more matter-of-fact comfortable kind of interaction. That is, they move to a level of involvement that is manageable. Surprisingly enough, some of these relationships settle into the kind of apathy that makes one wonder why they go on since there are no institutional obligations involved. But perhaps for some people sentiment and a quiescent kind of attachment are stronger than external social sanctions. Moreover, it is precisely because of their lowered intensity that these affairs can be carried on for a long time (sometimes as long as the primary relationship itself) without becoming threatening. Sometimes they are a primary factor in keeping a borderline primary relationship intact.

In one form of arrangement of this sort, the man is married, financially secure, and has no desire to see the affair evolve into a marriage since his marriage is quite tolerable and would be expensive to terminate. The woman is usually younger, either single or divorced, and desirous of a full commitment. The stability and endurance of the relationship is contingent on the woman's acceptance of the current limits of the involvement, while maintaining her fantasy of marriage in the future. "When my last child goes off to college" and "As soon as my wife becomes more independent" are the kinds of statements she hangs on to keep her hopes alive. Although there are a few exceptions, an affair of deep mutual involvement that continues over a number of years takes a mighty toll on both the lovers and the mate, or mates if both are in committed relationships. Again, the level of relationship involvement is an important consideration. Other factors (such as personal maturity) being equal, generally the closer the primary relationship, the greater the strain of the extraneous involvement. The adulterer's continual absences, excuses, lack of interest, and diminished sexual appetite will be sorely resented.

As an example of the direction this tension may take, consider the period when the unfaithful spouse attempts, whether out of guilt or compassion, to repair and revitalize their primary relationship. This saving effort may include attempts at talking things out, not the affair, but the voids in the relationship, the differences between the partners. He or she may suggest a long vacation together, "just the two of us, without the children." The affair-involved spouse may make overt or covert resolutions to be more loving, more tolerant, and more giving. Usually, these maneuvers don't work. Either the faithful spouse's suspicion, mistrust, and resentment are too intense to be dismissed by promises or the unfaithful spouse is still committed to the affair and is making a transparently feeble effort at reconciliation. In other instances, the adulterous mate is involved in self-deception. His efforts to talk things out and rekindle the primary relationship are a mask for the opportunity to criticize and emphasize shortcomings in his mate as justification for his divided loyalties.

As the relationship clashes increase in intensity, becoming more venomous and destructive, they affect the adulterous lovers. Rather than drawing closer, they find themselves at each other's throats. Celia's experience is common: "When Justin and I were feeling pressured or a conflict was raging at home, a great deal of tension and animosity developed between us. As the clashes increased in intensity and frequency at home, rather than consoling each other, we frequently made things worse. Our efforts to recapture earlier satisfaction paid off mostly when tensions at home were in remission."

ENDINGS

Celia and Justin had, at best, moderately close marriages; although they had several mutual interests and found their mates' company pleasant, if not stimulating, their marriages were not intimate. In contrast, their relationship with each other was extremely intimate. Unlike casual affairs, which may waste away and die quietly, affairs as intense as theirs die hard.

In the uninvolved casual affair, there is very little reward other than sexual pleasure. As alluring as this is, it is usually not enough to sustain a relationship. When the novelty wears off and the conquest is assured, interest begins to wane. Because of the lack of emotional involvement, parting is often somewhat painless, certainly not catastrophic, and without significant consequence to the primary relationship. Even when the meaning of the sexual act itself is highly significant to the individual, the breakup of a casual extra-relationship is not usually disruptive to the primary relationship.

Through a casual sexual encounter, an individual may become awakened to aspects of himself or herself or to aspects of the marital relationship that never surfaced before. For example, one woman found, after a brief sexual encounter, that she was more sexual and more orgasmic than she had ever dreamed possible. A man discovered that sexual acts his wife found distasteful and perverted were merely idiosyncratic. His extra-relationship sexual activity was an important experiential confirmation that his desires were not odd or "sick," as his wife had termed them. He felt better about himself and his sexuality as a result. Another person concluded after several affairs that her mate was the best all-around partner she could ever hope for. In these instances, if there is an effect on the primary relationship, it is not so much the extra-relationship as the extra-relationship experience that serves as the disruptive or enhancing force. When this is the case, breaking up the extraneous relationship is not usually a critical incident because it was the experience rather than the person that was significant.

If breaking up can be relatively painless in the casual encounter, the opposite is usually true in the grand amour where the person, rather than being incidental, is everything. Caught in a conflict between desire and obligation, between fulfillment and guilt, the adulterous mate suffers enormously and frequently manifests physical symptoms of his inner struggle. Torn between lover and mate, some individuals cannot sleep or sleep fitfully; others cannot eat or eat constantly; some take to excess drinking or to drugs; many become plagued by gastrointestinal and/or other psychosomatic disorders. Work suffers, household chores pile up, and the children are ignored. Frequently depression ensues. All of these symptoms deteriorate both the primary relationship and the affair. In such situations, it is imperative to make a decision, and paradoxically, very difficult to do so. It is an experience of suffering a loss that cannot be taken out of the shadows.

The experience was described by one man as sitting on a picket fence, feeling the painful inner probe but not daring to move. This man became withdrawn and preoccupied. His bills went unpaid, he began to snipe at old friends, and he considered leaving a well-paying position and moving. He wanted to start over; he wanted to kill himself; he didn't know what he wanted; he sought escape. He did not want to choose between his lover and his wife, yet he knew it was necessary for him to make a decision and act on it. In an emotion-filled conversation, Justin described his parting with Celia and its consequences for his marriage:

"I knew a choice had to be made. My marriage couldn't stand the conflict. Probably the most difficult aspect of this whole period was the necessity for concealing my pain. I was feeling so awful but I had to keep a lid on it because there was no way to account for these feelings to my family. I thought I would explode! While the decision to give up on my relationship with Celia in favor of my marriage relieved some of this agony, the loss and sorrow lasted for some time. There was also anger. Even though my wife's complaints and dissatisfactions about my being away from home so much and being preoccupied were very legitimate, I found myself blaming her for my dilemma. I realize that's crazy. She's a pretty decent person and she had a right to be dissatisfied. Things had been lousy between us during the affair.

"After my breakup with Celia, the problem was that I found myself acting in a way that would eventually destroy what was left of my marital relationship. That scared me; I would lose everything. But I went on, almost as if I didn't care. Between bouts of nastiness there were times when I would buy flowers and go through all sorts of romantic rituals. Then back to nastiness. This went on for about eight months before I settled down. If my wife wasn't such an exceptionally tolerant, easygoing person, there's no way our relationship would have lasted."

Of course, the conflict that an enduring high-involvement affair creates can go in another direction. It may lead to the dissolution of the marriage. Laura Greenstaff describes her experience:

"I was pretty unhappy in my first marriage. It was more a business arrangement than a relationship. We were so busy with our separate interests and responsibilities that we hardly noticed each other. There were· no real fights or even strong disagreements. On the contrary, there was a lack of any strong feelings. It's not that I expected heart palpitations every time I was in my husband's presence. I'm not that much of a romantic! But there was nothing. It was a very passive relationship, almost completely lacking in passion.

"My relationship with Harold, a business acquaintance of my husband, developed over a period of five years. As the years passed, it became more and more satisfying; more and more, my emotions became invested in Harold. We fussed over each other, there was a marvelous physical relationship, and, most important of all, we had emotional compatibility. It was beautiful. I don't regard it as dirty. Actually, when it seemed that Harold and I were seriously involved and meant to continue our involvement, I left my husband. I have no real regrets about my decision but I do feel very sorry and guilty for breaking up our home and inflicting pain on my family."

OLD LOVE OR NEW?

What accounts for the decision to stay with the marriage or to forsake it in favor of a new love? This is the type of question that cannot be answered fully; it is not something, like some of the issues in the previous pages, which is the subject of reliable research, it is more likely the fodder of novels. Even those doing the choosing are not able to unravel all the variables. For those who choose to stay with their mate, it may be a matter of security, financial and emotional connection. Guilt, obligation, loyalty, and duty to one's children or one's religion are also common factors. At a basic level, it may be that the primary relationship, although not fully satisfying, is not devoid of satisfaction. For even an incomplete and flawed relationship may, after the close scrutiny that conflict demands, become more practical and less romantic. This was the case with Justin. He recognized that although Celia is a more exciting woman than his wife, their relationship would prove unworkable in the long run; along with her vibrancy, Celia possessed a volatility and self-centeredness that would make a harmonious living arrangement very hard work, too hard for Justin's taste.

When the primary relationship is ended in favor of the affair, it is most likely because it was seriously deteriorating anyway and the lover promised, in addition to sexual satisfaction, emotional nourishment. Frequently, the affair-involved individual is strongly monogamous and became involved with a lover because of long-standing deprivation in the marriage. When love blossoms, the marriage rapidly becomes intolerable and the individual, in dissolving the marriage, is acting to restore his integrity as much as choosing greater satisfaction.

IMPLICATIONS

There you have it, affairs, like committed relationships, range from low to high involvement and, similarly, from neutral to grave in consequences. What kind of generalizations can we make from all of this? In summary, clinical experience suggests that if an individual is strongly monogamous, he or she is not likely to have an affair except out of sheer desperation. If this occurs, there is a high probability that if discovered, the marriage will end, or require intense treatment to save—although the motivation to do that, save the relationship—is not likely to be there. The likelihood of dissolution increases if the lover is suitable and available. In contrast, if an individual is not particularly restrained by the monogamous code, he or she will probably have more casual affairs—but meeting someone that develops into something more occasionally occurs.

If the primary relationship is not a close one, sometimes these affairs may be unnoticed and without consequence. They may even have the positive consequence of keeping a marriage that is satisfactory in most respects alive and intact. If the primary relationship is a close one, a strain is likely to develop even if the affairs are casual, how great a strain depends on the sensitivity of the faithful mate and how much time the extraneous involvements take from the primary relationship.

Of course, even if the affair is casual and the lover is not valued, the experience itself may have a personal impact with consequences for the long-term relationship. These consequences are very complex and range from destructive to enhancing. The grand amour, the deep involvement, the all-encompassing affair, is a paradox; a once-in-a-lifetime experience, it is also agonizing and the riskiest of all. In the close, involved primary relationship, it is nearly always a disaster, a head-on collision. In relationships that are not close, it is likely to be a continuing source of conflict, if not the beginning of the end.

Sound Thinking and Smart Moves

1. There are critical moments in a love relationship and many people get it wrong. Hurt feelings, misunderstandings, and frustrations are part of relationships. Rather than finding an effective way to talk these issues out, too many couples withdraw. Withdrawal leaves a distance in the relationship that makes infidelity more tempting.

2. Using the excuse of "We're not that close anyway," as a basis for beginning an affair is a popular lie we tell ourselves to rationalize an affair, but like other lies we tell ourselves it is in the service of giving ourselves permission, in this case for breaching the trust of our partner.

3. Thinking that one's partner will soon get over the discovery of a low-involvement affair is a convenient and self-serving rationalization. In actuality, most people in a low-involvement primary relationship are completely devastated when their partner's affair is discovered. It may be more about a sense of abandonment and a sensitive trust history then the loss of their mate, but nonetheless devastating.

Chapter 3

LUST AND BEYOND: MOTIVATIONS FOR INFIDELITY

SEARCHING FOR . . . WHAT?

Why did this happen? What was this about? Was it about love? The reason for an affair is a question that betrayed partners may contemplate for a long time. As we have seen, infidelity literature has reported on the different factors behind being unfaithful such as education level, personality, opportunity, attachment style, income level as well as employment, race, culture, religion, and marital satisfaction. Drigotas et al. (1999) divided these proposed motives driving infidelity into five categories: sexuality, emotional satisfaction, social context, attitudes-norms, and revenge/hostility. Research has also focused on the desire for sexual variety as a common basis for engaging in infidelity (Johnson, 1970; Roscoe et al., 1988).

Studies have also focused on marital satisfaction (Buss & Shackelford, 1997b). Dissatisfaction with the marital or cohabiting primary relationship is one possible motivation. It is difficult, however, to determine the exact connection between relationship dissatisfaction and extra-relationship affairs. Given that much research into infidelity is retrospective, this data is not helpful in determining which came first, the affair or the relationship problems. For example, one study's results showed that individuals who had engaged in an affair felt the affair was caused by relationship problems, while their partners believed that their relationship problems were caused by the affair (Spanier & Margolis, 1983).

Social contextual factors, as noted earlier, often were related to education level, personality, attachment style, income level as well as employment, race, and culture. The literature also demonstrates that attitudes toward infidelity (partners with liberal sexual attitudes) are more likely to engage in infidelity (Hansen, 1987; Prins et al., 1993). Finally, infidelity as revenge is also a common reason for being unfaithful among couples (Buss & Shackelford, 1997a; Greene, Lee, & Lustig, 1974).

So, what motivates people to seek extra-relationship sexual experiences? It appears that the research is as varied as extra-relationship experiences. Love, of course, is the most popularized reason, even if it is lust masquerading as love. On screen and in novels, love is portrayed as taking us unaware, capturing us, and causing us, as if shot by Cupid's arrow, to fall helplessly into another's arms. In real life, though, researchers and investigative interviewers find love a rather uncommon basis of infidelity.

What, then, does account for the proliferation of extra-relationship sex? There is, of course, no single or simple answer; each extra-relationship affair is the result of a complex interplay of forces. Members of the psychological professions are divided as to whether neurotic personality characteristics or normal and even healthy traits are primarily responsible for adulterous behavior. Some psychologists and psychiatrists who take the former position believe that people are adulterous because they were conditioned by childhood experiences to be unable to form deep commitments, or because they are so immature that they can acknowledge no limit to their needs, or can acquire no realistic perspective on what to expect from a long-term relationship.

Curiously enough, analytic-oriented psychology/psychiatry professionals, those supposedly responsible for unleashing the view that sexuality is inherent and perhaps drives much of our behavior, take a harsh view of affairs. They generally regard practically all extra-relationship activity as symptomatic of pathological personality traits such as psychosexual immaturity, narcissism, character disorder, attachment disorders, and oedipal conflict. The evidence they present for their view comes from clinical practice with impotent men seeking potency; nonassertive, browbeaten mates who feel like worthy people only outside their marriages; couples embroiled in long-standing hostility who use cheating as a weapon; men and women who do not feel worthy of respect unless they are continually "proving" they are by new sex-love conquests; and pathologically insecure, jealous husbands and wives who drive their mates into another's arms by their constant badgering.

Of course, as has been frequently pointed out about Freud's and other psychoanalysts' conclusions about human behavior, it is not entirely legitimate for a therapist to investigate the lives of individuals who seek help for a particular disturbance and then make sweeping generalizations about the motives of all people. Yet, it is indisputable that there are a good number of neurotically based, self-defeating reasons for extra-relationship affairs, and there are also some drivers of affairs that are not immersed in psychological pathology, even if underhanded and disruptive. Here, a discussion of some of the more common motives, albeit an incomplete listing since the various motives could probably fill an entire volume on the subject.

VARIETIES OF SELF-DECEPTION: EGO BOOSTING

An affair that is engaged in to avoid personal or marital problems, or to do something to a third party (such as an affair of revenge), or for ego bolstering (going from one relationship to another with the purpose of enhancing one's feelings of potency and power) is self-defeating. It is self-defeating in the same manner that heroin addiction is: it simply doesn't work in the long run and is not only a fake solution; it is likely to make things worse. In short, the relief is temporary; the problem remains unsolved, or indeed, is complicated by the attempted solution.

When Dan and Barbara first married, he thought, "She has everything." She took away his anxiety in being with a woman, did most of the talking, brought home a terrific executive salary, and, by her social adeptness, determined their day-to-day activities.

Initially, Dan felt some of Barbara's super competence would "rub off" on him. Instead, shortly after they were married, Dan felt that his inadequacies were highlighted by Barbara's attainments; he felt less brilliant than she, awkward with people in general, and frustrated by his inability to progress in his career as rapidly as his wife. Barbara, for her part, was content that Dan was responsible, considerate, and a loving father. She loved him and did not make the kinds of torturous comparisons that Dan did, and on several occasions she reassured him of this. Unfortunately, Dan would not accept what he viewed as a one-up/one-down relationship. He was sure that she and their entire social circle undervalued him and that sooner or later his wife would admit her unhappiness with his inferiority and run off with someone who was her equal. "Why would she want to continue living with me? Realistically, I don't measure up to her business associates; I just haven't made it."

Dan, in a futile effort to buffer himself from his wife's and their friends' "rejection," had a number of affairs with women who he knew couldn't measure up to him. He felt that because they had done poorly in life, they would think him rather terrific.

"I needed these affairs. I always felt I needed shoring up. The only thing I was ever sure of about myself was that I was good-looking. Nothing else. I had no confidence in myself as a person of intelligence. What intellectual veneer I had was polished onto me by Barbara. I don't even have confidence in myself as a lover. So I go thrashing about, always looking for reassurance."

Some, like Dan, are so perfectionist in the demands they place on themselves and so self-demeaning when they do not live up to these demands that they cannot bear to face themselves or their mates, who know them with all their inadequacies. They condemn themselves for not being up to par as housekeepers, athletes, parents, lovers, or monetary providers. Male-female roles being what they are in our society, men who are adulterous because of personal feelings of inadequacy frequently view themselves as incompetent because of professional or business failures and think they can somehow compensate for these defects by sexual conquests; while wives who are adulterous as a result of their feelings of worthlessness commonly believe they are boring, non-contributive, and sexually inferior, and that the affair will somehow transform them into being exciting and amorous.

The pattern is, first, to set up unrealistic demands that deprive us of our self-acceptance, and then to seek relief in affairs (or alcohol, drugs, or compulsive job hopping). The purpose is diversion and temporary relief from discomfort. The relief is merely palliative and ultimately self-defeating, for the problem exists in the person's head, in the insistence that in order to be an acceptable human being, to like yourself, you have to excel. This perfectionist, unrealistic demand is what needs rethinking; the affairs, drinking, and other compensatory behaviors only evade the real issue and often make things worse. Sure, a person may be comfortable while doing these things but the comfort is short-lasting and may be at the expense of personal and relationship well-being. The question for those caught in this cycle is, what do you want: temporary relief or the longer-lasting, life-promoting goal of working things out with yourself and your relationship?

AVOIDANCE

Just as extra-relationship sex was used by Dan to boost his sagging ego, it can also be used to avoid or detract from other psychological issues. Rather than face and eventually work out relationship, social, or work problems, the affair can be used as an easy way out. It seems easier to run from affair to affair or to immerse oneself in an intense affair than to confront a drab, meaningless existence. A case in point involves Carol, a very bright woman in her early thirties, who has been married for six years to an engineer. Carol had quit college after one semester, because she found the work too demanding of her time and energy. She then dabbled for short periods in photography and painting. While she was doing well in these areas, she felt encouraged and enthusiastic. However, as soon as things became more difficult, she gave up.

The same pattern occurred with tennis, an attempt to go back to school, music lessons, and a host of other activities; there was short-lived enthusiasm, then decline, and eventual termination of the activity. Each time, when the activity became a bit too difficult, Carol's interest began to wane. As a result of her attitude—"If things get hard I won't be able to measure up, so I'd better give up"—Carol had no vital absorbing interests in life. Because she refused to work at finding major goals that would give more meaning to her life, she rather easily fell into a series of affairs to forget the aimlessness of her existence. As Carol explained:

"After two years and numerous affairs, I'm not any happier; if anything, my life is even more of a mess. I've neglected my children and my husband. I've acted in ways that I don't respect. It's very difficult to acknowledge that I've been wasting my life. As a child I can recall being told, "Oh Carol, you're so bright, you'll do well at whatever you try." The pressure! Knowing that it was expected of me made doing well an obsession. Even if I did well, keeping it up put an enormous strain on me. I remember an incident that occurred out west. I was training to be a race car driver. Imagine, I was hoping to be among the few competitive woman drivers. I was enrolled in a well-known school for professional drivers. One day at the start of a practice race I heard that several of the other drivers, instead of being amateurs, were real pros who had stopped by to shape up. I became so frightened that I just looked absolutely straight ahead. I glued my eyes to a spot about five feet ahead of the car, and as we moved out at the start of the race, I just maintained this concentrated stare directly in front of the car. Well, about midway through the race I dared to look back and noticed I was way out ahead of the field, pros and all! Immediately, I took the escape route off the track. If I had won that race, could you imagine the expectations people would have had for me next time out? I quit racing soon after that.

"My affairs, as I see them now, were evasions. I blamed my marriage; I blamed my robust sexuality. I realize now that I wasn't merely seeking an adventurous relief from marital boredom or even feeling particularly lustful. Actually, my marriage had been quite satisfactory. I can't blame that. No, when I get right down to it, it's my personal problem that has led me to be so compulsively adulterous. I suppose it was a desperate attempt to fill up a life that I feel is shitted up. Except it didn't really work. Here I am two years later after lots of screwing, still screwed up. I still have no goals. I am still empty, except now I've jeopardized my marriage and I don't know if there's enough left to salvage."

As Carol herself recognized about her affairs, all with men who promised her everything but delivered nothing but heartache, she had gained practically nothing from these relationships but preoccupation. She had no constructive goal, she was merely filling up her time, and any long-term, organized purpose she might have developed was no nearer to fruition.

Another type of avoidance that frequently motivates extra-relationship sex is the refusal to acknowledge that one is growing older. It is no secret that our society is obsessed with youth. Youth has been made synonymous with beauty, vitality, gaiety, and idealism, all that is good, pure, and, especially, joyful. Age has become a specter to be feared and a process to be fought. This adulation of youth touches us all; we are exposed to it continually. Whether our youth has been joyous and carefree or not (and for most of us it was a difficult period), the distortions of time may cause us to remember it as one long "good time." If, on the other hand, we remember those adolescent years with pain and as a time of loneliness and rejection, we may long for a youth we feel we missed. Thus, an exciting affair maybe thought of as a means of living the carefree youth we missed or of reliving one that is more a fantasy than a memory.

Jerry, a man approaching fifty, was, as a teenager, very shy and generally inhibited, particularly with girls. He had terrible acne and always worried that girls would find him unattractive. As he got older, his complexion cleared and he married Lisa, the first girl he dated. Jerry was twenty-four years old. Lisa was a calm, reserved woman who Jerry felt loved him very much.

Regarding his many affairs, Jerry, while studying his reflection in an office window, put it thus: "I didn't want to have affairs. The last thing I'd want to do is to hurt Lisa. Yet I've felt compelled to see other women. I feel I've missed something in my life. I've lost my youth; I'll be fifty next month! If it wasn't shyness, it was making ends meet, always something. Now I want to make up for lost time. The first time I had an affair was so exciting, secret meetings, great sex all afternoon, dangerous, mysterious. I felt like a young man again, alive! I don't want to be just another aging, weary commuter. It would be very painful for me to end up like my father, who, as far back as I can remember, was a dull, paunchy, TV addict who had just given up. That's not for me! Affairs are my youth connection. I need them to keep me alive, and I admit this type of renewal is very important to me."

Certain ages have taken on almost symbolic meaning in our society. Thirteen represents the threshold onto adolescence, twenty-one signifies the rights of adulthood, and age forty for some women and fifty for some men are given a significance that has no necessary relationship to reality. Overnight these women, particularly if they are not coupled, see themselves turning old, losing their vitality, and, above all, their attractiveness. They spend hours searching for and worrying about wrinkles and compulsively try to offset the aging process so that potential husbands will not lose interest in them.

For Jerry and for many men, age fifty seems to carry the same significance but with the added complication that they fear it marks the decline in their virility. The so-called roving forties, now extended to the fifties, is a reflection of this phenomenon. Some husbands, fearing a loss of sexual vitality with the onset of middle age, set out to "prove" they are still young lovers. Interestingly, various studies, including the reports of Kinsey and his associates, have shown that virility does not take a noticeable drop at age forty—and that was decades ago, when men had a shorter life span—but if a man believes his potency will drastically diminish then, it probably will, and his attempts to restore it through sexual affairs will probably be futile.

In another conversation, Jerry voiced the sentiments suggested earlier. He said, "I was raised in a family where it was evident that after the first four decades of life, there was no joyful living. I was taught by my dad's example, and I foolishly believed that at middle age you might as well curl up and die. My affairs are largely an overreaction to that environment."

This is the crux of the compulsive drive to recapture a youth that never was—the belief that youth is the last opportunity to experience joy and excitement and that the later years of life and committed relationships are doomed to be routine, boring, and filled with long dead dreams. It bears a psychological similarity to the strong fear of death so many of us experience; we fear we may die without ever having lived. Compulsive adultery is a very limited solution to this dilemma. How we choose to perceive our age will determine whether we dig an ever deeper rut while trying to relive our lost youth through sexual conquest, or whether we continually learn more ways to live our lives to the fullest with an insight not typically available to youth.

HOSTILITY

One of the more common self-defeating motives for an affair is revenge. Typically, one of the relationship partners holds many hidden grudges against the other; he or she has a lot of unexpressed anger against the spouse. The anger may be denied; even the fact that a problem exists may be denied. The other partner is typically willing to show anger and does and is manipulative in dealing with his or her "passive" mate. The withdrawal of the passively angry partner is a result of having no effective outlet for communicating anger. He or she seems to be unable or unwilling to show anger toward his or her mate either to place strong limits on what will and will not be tolerated or to clear the air between them.

Perhaps even more important than the lack of open, angry communication by the withdrawing mate is the absence of appropriate assertive behavior. He does not seem to be able to express his own likes, or his mate is able, by manipulation, to prevent him from acting on his own desires. The passive mate seems dreadfully lacking in the ability to tell his or her partner calmly (or not so calmly) of his or her displeasure with the way things are going between them. Instead, the "silent" mate withdraws and fantasizes ways to "get back."

Roslyn, a very attractive, intense woman with a twelve-year-old daughter, has been married twice and has been adulterous in both her marriages. The first time she used extra-relationship sex mainly to find a man who would rescue her from a marriage that had deteriorated. Once married to a gyne-cologist, the man who had taken her out of her first unhappy marriage, she continued to use extra-relationship sex because, she said, her second husband took her for granted and put her very low on his list of priorities.

"Being a product of my times, I use extra-relationship sex as a weapon. My husband works long hours when he really doesn't have to, and I resent it. When he comes home, he is preoccupied. He wants to watch television, read, sleep, or go on his boat. That boat is driving me crazy. I don't want to compete with a goddam boat! I feel he would choose that boat over me without an instant of hesitation. I don't feel married. It seems he regards me as a con-venience. When he is attentive, it is often in a belittling and critical manner; he makes me feel stupid and ridiculous. One time I was relining the shelves in one of the closets very meticulously because I like things to be perfect and beautiful, and he nagged me something awful and called me a fool for wasting my time on something no one would ever see. So, either he pesters me or he ignores me, and I don't have the courage to tell him I don't like him doing that, at least not with the rage I feel. I simply have lovers. And then, when my husband continues to ignore me, to take me for granted, or comes on with his criticisms, I sit back, smile inside, and say to myself, 'You're not so hot, you fool.' That's my revenge!"

Roslyn sought revenge for her husband's inattention. A somewhat different example of a hostility-motivated affair involves Mr. and Mrs. Herbert Blake, a prosperous suburban couple who have been married for fifteen years. They had two teenaged children and were socially popular. Everybody thought they had a fine marriage. Mr. Blake was an executive with a substantial income. His wife was well-dressed, played excellent bridge, and did more than her share of local charity work. Both were considered socially desirable, well-informed conversationalists in their set, but at home Mr. Blake rarely said much. To keep the peace, he went along with whatever his wife wanted.

One day shortly after leaving for an all-day charity event, Mrs. Blake returned home unexpectedly for the raffle tickets left on the kitchen table and discovered Herbert in bed with another woman. At first, she was incredulous, then horrified. In the marital crisis that followed, Mrs. Blake learned that the "silent treatment" she had received all these years was not cooperation or strength but hostility camouflaged by phony and misleading compliance. Mr. Blake admitted that he had never leveled with his wife, never clearly commu-nicated his feelings about the way she dominated most of the family decisions. Though it riled him to no end when she decided what they should do to "have fun" or to "be creative," almost invariably he went along with her ideas. On the few occasions when he did protest mildly—always without making the true depth of his feelings clear—he found that his wife became even more asser-tive. So he became quieter. As he put it:

"I felt it undignified to get in there and really let her have it. I grew up in a family with a lot of screaming. I remember the hurts, the insults, the pain, and meanness very vividly. I didn't want that in my life. I didn't want to get embroiled in the kind of rage my parents expressed. Yet being dominated, bossed around, feeling like a doormat, wasn't my cup of tea either. I chose an affair with a particularly passive woman, by the way, as an equalizer. Taking her to the house, of course, was stupid. Although if I'm going to be brutally honest, I must admit to having mixed emotions about being caught, part of it being, 'Good, you bastard, at last you can unmistakably see you are not dealing with the village idiot!' I feel curiously relieved."

Both Roslyn and Herbert Blake share a common deceptive belief: It isn't "gentlemanly," it isn't "feminine," to express emotionally and firmly dissatis-faction and annoyance. It isn't nice. It isn't mature. This is supposed to be the age of reason, so we must always act civilized and reasonable. Only we don't always feel civilized and reasonable! Ideally, relationship communication is best if conducted in a harmonious manner but this need not always be so. Shrieking and yelling, accusations and counteraccusations, nasty comments and snide retorts, and other unpleasant ways of interacting are in many cases the best a beleaguered couple can do in the beginning, at least until they learn to communicate more effectively. Stewing and being passive-aggressive is often worse.

Despite the fact that after the first few minutes brawling becomes counter-productive and makes things worse, it can also be very revealing and useful in the initial heat. "You don't love me anymore. You never put your hands on me except when you have sex on your mind. You never do anything to help me, but if Phyl-lis Taft wants a hand with her packages, that's a different story. You can go to hell as far as I'm concerned!" This is a very important message that perhaps could only be delivered, at the time, in sobs and shouts. Sometimes any kind of com-munication that deals with what is wrong with an ailing relationship is likely to be better than no communication at all. In fact, researchers have found that couples who regard their relationship as satisfactory actually fight more than couples who are unhappy in their relationship—but they fight better and make up better as is discussed in *The Marriage Clinic* (Gottman & Levenson, 1999).

For some couples who do not communicate about the things that are really bothering them, a less-than-desirable approach may be a better start than no start. That is, some beginning is better than none at all, especially if there is awareness of what is going on and if the bickering is viewed as a primary stage of communication that can develop into a more harmonious dialogue. In fact, the path to effective interaction will likely be helped if couples can approach each other after emotions have cooled, like the next day or so, and do two things in a follow-up interaction: (1) apologize for aspects of the earlier interaction that were egregious and (2) validate the other person's view, bearing in mind validating is not agreeing, it is simply demonstrating an understanding of the other's view. One thing is certain: an affair is not the answer. It will merely give one person an unfair advantage over the other and serve as a diversion from real intimacy.

Affairs of resentment may also be a form of rebellion in a relationship that at base is solid. The rebellion in these cases is against monogamy, the grievance being that it forces one to give up the pleasures of the single life in return for the special fulfillment only a marriage or a similar long-term commitment can provide. Carl is twenty-eight; he has been married for five years.

"When my wife was in her sixth month of pregnancy, it hit me, I'm stuck; I'm really married. We had been married for several years, but I never felt trapped, or as if I was really married. There were no real responsibilities. With a child coming, I felt really scared. Was I doing the right thing? Was marriage really for me? Up until then I had never really had to consider those questions. I guess in the back of my mind I always figured I could get out. With the pregnancy, I saw it as too late—what kind of heel would leave his wife in her sixth month? I couldn't live with that, but I also felt, for the first time, really tied down. What a lousy sense of timing. When Cathy flew to Minnesota to visit her aunt, I remember thinking maybe the plane will crash and I'll be freed. It was a horrible thought. I was ashamed that I could even think such a thing. Although I was doing a lot of bickering, I always considered Cathy a friend, a very decent, giving, and accommodating person. I was beside myself.

"My affairs, and there were many, made the statement, 'I won't be restrained by any societal rule,' and closer to the heart of the matter, 'Cathy, damn it, how could you do this to me? I'll show you that I can't be contained.' The whole thing was unreasonable. I failed to take responsibility for my own actions. I was into blaming. Paradoxically, when I realized the choice to adventure sexually or not was mine, that it was up to me to decide, when I really felt that I no longer had any desire to stray. It wasn't sex all along; it was the severe proscription that I wouldn't accept."

UNSELECTIVE SELECTION

Unlike Carl, who had chosen a basically compatible mate but perhaps at too early an age, some individuals choose poorly. With them, it is not so much the affair itself that is unwise but the choice of the primary partner that elevates the affair to such status. Edith, a passionate, earthy woman already once divorced, explains her affairs as a matter of sexual deprivation:

"My honeymoon was a nightmare, an absolute, utter nightmare. He just seemed to disintegrate under the pressure of having to make love. Making love just didn't seem to be his forte. I really hated going to bed with him after a while and only did it because I felt ashamed just to masturbate, but actually being sexually involved with him was a turnoff. He'd touch me, get me all aroused, then enter and finish one second later. When I just met him I figured that after we were married, he'd relax and get over it slowly. As it turned out, things got worse instead of better. A lot of the time, he couldn't even get it up. I had to have some relief or I thought I'd go out of my mind."

The point here is that Edith, who had had plenty of premarital experience and numerous affairs between marriages should have known better. Sex is very important to her, yet she married a man who had sexual difficulties. She made this mistake because of her strong need for a passive and inadequate man she could take care of. Unfortunately, she found she was not a healer. Eventually her husband discovered her affairs and left her. Edith's situation has variations on a theme: often a woman enters a relationship hoping her partner will change and a man enters hoping she won't change. Typically, both end up wrong; unhappily, she changes, and he doesn't.

For all of these people—those who enter the world of extra-relationship affairs as a shortsighted solution to emotional or relationship difficulties—for them the affair is seen as proof of personal power, vindictiveness, or reassurance. Sensual pleasure is not what these people are seeking in each new conquest; they want to alleviate the pain in aspects of their lives or relationships that they find insufferable. Rather than repair or leave a seriously ailing relationship or work on their problems, they engage in affairs that typically are shallow, brief, and numerous to the point of compulsive promiscuity. The needs these affairs satisfy can be subsumed under the heading "self-indulgence," looking for a solution that will likely add to the problem.

This is not to say that when someone has an affair or even a series of affairs for unwise, self-deceptive reasons, it is always a frustrating counterproductive experience. That would be too simplistic. Some people begin with primarily neurotic motivation but then discover some very important things about themselves in the course of their infidelities. This happened to Roslyn, who initially sought revenge in her affairs.

"After seeking comfort in a score of affairs and finding it only very briefly in each, I finally entered therapy and slowly discovered that in both my marriages I had chosen a powerful and punishing man very much like my father, and hence I had neither been able to fight back nor walk out on my own. After two years of therapy, I divorced, spent a stretch of time being single, and then was remarried, this time to a totally different type of man. Truthfully, my affairs were mostly a waste of time, but not completely. I feel that my experience with many men is what first sparked the realization that it was me—not the man—who was the problem. That's when I decided on therapy. I don't know if I would have come to the same point without the affairs. I could simply have become resigned to my miserable fate."

PLURALIST SEXUAL DESIRES

Just as extra-relationship desires and actions can be exaggerated, compulsive, and self-deceptive, they can also be ordinary, normal, and even indices of growth. Generally, an affair that is not pathological is one engaged in for its own sake. The individual seeks primarily neither to hurt another person nor to compensate for felt inadequacy and does not feel compelled to carry out or continue the behavior if it endangers a valued relationship.

Perhaps the most frequent cause of infidelity is the simple, natural, normal feeling of boredom, sexual, emotional, or both. As new research has been conducted and described in the *New York Times* article noted previously, by nature some of us are varietists. For those, a committed relationship particularly over an extended period of time smothers their varietist inclinations. That this natural varietist tendency of human beings is well within the normal range of behaviors and is not necessarily indicative of emotional or sexual disturbance is attested to by many outstanding authorities.

For example, while research has been competed recently noting a genetic predisposition to seek out risk, excitement, and adventure, it is preceded by animal studies reviewed by Kinsey and his associates. They observed that male rats, monkeys, and bulls who had been observed to copulate repeatedly until they became exhausted and stopped when restricted to one partner, would, if new females were offered to them, become remarkably restored and begin copulating with the new partners with nearly all the energy and excitement they originally had. Kinsey, considering these experiments along with a review of the anthropological evidence, concluded that the varietist urge is part of the mammalian nerve heritage and man is also subject to this biological influence. The male human being would, nearly always, behave pluralistically were it not for social restraints.

As for the female, in *Sexual Behavior in the Human Female*, Kinsey and his associates write, "We have already observed that the anatomy and physiology of sexual response and orgasm do not show differences between the sexes that might account for the differences in their sexual responses." They conclude that the female's somewhat weaker polygamous tendency is probably a matter of social conditioning rather than instinct.

Two outstanding and highly respected sex researchers, Drs. Clellan S. Ford and Frank A. Beach (1951), provide evidence on this point: In a summary of the sexual patterns in 185 societies, they point out that wherever there is no double standard in sexual matters, and extra-relationship liaisons are tolerated, women are as eager and ready for variety as men. The desire for novelty and variety is apparently inherent in most human beings; long-term exclusivity with a sexual-emotional companion is not an innate human need but a culturally induced one. Since we are by nature varietists, more and less, and by social cultural upbringing exclusivists, we are frequently in conflict. And this is why many of us—even the normal and the satisfactorily married—are so sorely tempted and sometimes act on our desires for novelty and change. Sara, a suburban college instructor, age thirty-seven, mother of one, puts it this way:

"I love my husband very much. I love making love to him. I wouldn't want to live with anyone else. And I don't have to have an occasional affair. . . . Just as I'm sure I could live on a limited nutrient diet and stay healthy, I could live within the confines of my marriage and stay healthy. Admittedly, though, there is a degree of monotony that I see no reason to endure. I don't regard my very occasional affair as cheating anybody of anything. I am not taking inordinate time away from my family nor am I particularly preoccupied during these periods, which are infrequent and usually brief. My sporadic encounters may even contribute to the marriage. The liveliness and emotional satisfaction I derive definitely feeds back into the marriage in a positive way. As a matter of fact, it may be that during an affair I am more sexy and affectionate with my husband rather than less, as most people would think."

SEX/AFFECTION DEPRIVATION

Many of us have the security of sexual sameness and would like occasional variety. Some of us, though, do not have this security. That is, some men and women are sexually deprived either temporarily or permanently. They may be separated because of lengthy business trips or other obligations; one mate may be in exceptionally poor health for an extended period; or one may have a substantially stronger libido than the other. In these circumstances, the deprived mate may develop feelings of resentment that can easily disrupt a relationship that in most other aspects is quite satisfactory.

Lyle is an architect who has been married to Ginger for fourteen years. He is very successful in his field and has won several professional citations. He describes his marriage as "right out of the storybooks—we are both loving and considerate to each other." Lyle characterizes his wife as "a typical, home-loving soul, very family-oriented." They live in a suburb. He commutes each day while she gardens, refinishes antiques, and prepares gourmet meals. They have three children. Lyle describes his affairs this way:

"I become involved in affairs as a supplement to my marriage. I simply have much more desire for intimacy and much more sexual energy than my wife could possibly absorb. To deny myself the affairs and to direct the resulting frustration at my wife might be more honest, but very cruel. My wife has an open attitude toward sex and would probably not be shattered if she found out about my affairs. Yet she prides herself on meeting most of my needs and would be hurt. I am especially careful about this. I seek out women who are, to some degree, unfulfilled at home, yet who are strongly committed to their families. They feel safe having an affair with me because of my commitment and I feel safe with them.

"One of the things I value most about my extra relationship liaisons is getting to know another person on an emotional level. Not that it is always intimate just because we have sex, or that it can't be if we don't, but there have been disclosures in some of my relationships that have contributed to me as a person. My wife, who overall I would choose over any of the other women I've known, does not have the instability, the outright craziness that some of these women possess.

"It seems that there are advantages and disadvantages to any life choice. I wanted a woman who was stable, not neurotically demanding, and, of course, loving. Ginger is all of these things. An occasional fling with someone like Marie, the Greenwich Village poetess with long black hair and electrifying eyes, is fantastic, though. She is nothing like Ginger. She does not want a family commitment, and living with her would be nothing short of a disaster, and Jana is wise enough to know that. Is she crazy? Not really, just not made to live with another person, but in bed she is like a volcano, erupting to the touch. I don't want to give that up unless it will interfere with my primary commitment to Ginger and the children."

DIMINISHMENT OF INNOCENCE

It certainly can be hotly argued, that some avoid an affair, not out of love or ethics. Just as the decision in favor of an affair is often for inappropriate or unwise reasons, so may the refusal of an affair be less than noble. Many persons avoid an affair because they need to feel innocent or because they are extremely dependent on their spouses. These attitudes are appropriate to growing children and it seems many people fail to achieve adult autonomy. Those who are caught in this impasse may have an affair in order to perform as "bad child" or may refuse an affair in order to perform as "good child." In either case, their behavior is immature not because of the act or the refusal to act but because of the basis on which the decision is made.

The need to feel innocent, to remain the "good child," is not an uncommon phenomenon in our society. People have a need to feel innocent in direct proportion to their lack of maturity. The process of fulfilling one's sexual potential, because of the special meaning given to sex in our society, is a continuing story of the loss of innocence. Roberta, a woman of thirty-three, recalls her experiences in this regard:

"My relationship with my parents as a youngster was pretty good. They were sophisticated and highly-educated people who never really told me what to do, but there was a very strong emotional connection there and it was very important to me to please them. When I reached late adolescence and began to masturbate, I felt trusting of them and discussed it openly. I recall them being pleased by this. And, in turn, I was pleased by their acceptance. As I see it now, though, my confession was not merely an act of openness and trust, but a struggle to regain my lost innocence. In actuality, the discussion with my parents was aimed at getting their approval. I was not autonomous enough to come to terms about this by myself, or through my peers.

"My premarital sexual experiences had the same tone. They were, in important respects, similar to my adolescent struggles. I did not have intercourse previous to marriage but I did practically everything else. Again, I saw not 'going all the way' as retaining my 'goodness.' One time, involved in very heavy petting, I became so sexually excited that I got scared and began to bawl. I cried because I felt driven to complete the act but yet wouldn't for fear I would lose something. This was about three months before I married and the man involved was my fiancé!

"In my marriage, the principal deterrent to having an affair was the overriding need to feel innocent, to be a 'good girl.' To have an affair would be to lose that innocence. For one thing, I could not, that is, I would choose not to be open about the affair. I could not share this aspect of my life with my husband. I thought about this and about the things that have occurred in the past with my sexuality. As a result, I decided to have an affair. It was brief and in itself not particularly terrific. My husband is a more considerate lover and a brighter, more exciting person than this other man, which I could have predicted because my husband, Ron has so much going for him. But I regard the affair as a very important, positive growth experience.

"First, I no longer bear the burden of the necessity to be innocent. I guess I could have come to this same conclusion without the affair; I could have worked the whole thing out in my head, but it just didn't seem enough. It could too easily have been another rationalization to remain the 'good girl.' Second, I found that intimacy does not require complete disclosure of one's thoughts, feelings, and actions. Total openness is unrealistic. Each mature individual—and this is the point—carries with them some experiences that they need not share. I can now live with this comfortably. This type of privacy has no relation to shame. Actually, it is just the opposite; the compulsion 'to tell all' sometimes seems to be an effort to remove shame and guilt. The affair and its implications for me have been an affirmation; my independence, my autonomy as a human being, have been expanded. I prize that experience."

SEXUAL CURIOSITY

Closely related to a loss of innocence is sexual curiosity. Although an increasing number of people today have affairs between the time one relationship ends by divorce, break-up, or death of a spouse and another begins, many mature adults (especially women) have had very few sex partners in their entire lives. Some of these people, both men and women, are shamed by this. They think to themselves, "What's the matter with me; in this enlightened age everyone should have varied sexual experiences." It is the shame that drives them to adultery. Others, including those who are happily married and who would never consider breaking up their homes, may be motivated not by the false dictum of "Thou Must Be Sexually Experienced" but by simple curiosity. Husbands and wives who engage in affairs out of sexual curiosity may not constitute a high percentage, but those who consider it and are sometimes tempted to do it are far from rare.

Josephine married Eli when she was nineteen years old. They live in a small conservative community and have been together nine years. Their first child was born after two years of marriage, and the second a year later. For the past several years, Josephine has been too preoccupied with two preschool young-sters to give serious thought to her occasional sexual fantasies involving other men. Now that both children are in school, she finds herself more acutely aware of her sexual curiosity. Aside from teenage petting, Eli is the only man with whom she has had sexual experience. In conversation with Josephine, she stated that although she is quite tempted to experiment with another man, Eli would be absolutely destroyed if he found out. "Realistically," she added, "in this community the chances of being caught are pretty high." Rather than take the chance and risk Eli's emotional upset, Josephine has decided, at least for the time being, to stay with her fantasies.

Josephine's desire, as she described it, did not seem self-deceptive. Nor would her acting on that desire be neurotic had her life circumstances been different. Her choice not to act appeared quite legitimate, that is, regardless of the legitimacy of her motives, her marriage probably would not have survived discovery and that was too heavy a price to pay. Perhaps most striking was her closing remark to me: "I do not feel cheated by my choice. I needn't satisfy my wants just because I would like to. I can stand not having it all."

DECIPHERING THE DESIRE

Extra-relationship sexual encounters usually are multi-motivated. That is, although we have been speaking of extra-relationship sexual behavior as though it were singularly motivated by a need to be assured or a need to impress or desire for closeness or for love or for variety, in reality it is usually a combination of these motives that propels an individual. Indeed, research supports that individuals who engage in these relationships report motivations that are relatively varied and complex. Further, they cannot be easily gender-typed (Omarzu et al., 2012).

Determining our motives, then, or the motives of an adulterous mate is no easy task. Indeed, to complicate matters, situational factors also influence an individual. For example, a relatively happy, emotionally stable man might never become unfaithful in a conservative community where the pressures to conform are strong. The same man, even if not particularly desirous of extra-relationship sex, might, if freed from external controls by a permissive community and a permissive wife, may act on his low-level urge.

So, how does one go about answering the question, "Why am I doing this?" or, in reflecting on the case of an adulterous mate, "Why did it happen?" First, it would be best to think in terms of primary motives rather than *the* motive. Additionally, a careful consideration of outside circumstances is helpful. These may range from the type of community one lives in, the influences of friends, to such things as career setbacks, life transitions (e.g., the last child going off to school and leaving a housewife suddenly alone), and serious relationship strife.

Honest, persistent questioning is probably the most useful tack whether considering internal factors or external conditions. "Am I finding my relationship boring because I want to find it so in order to excuse my extra-relationship ventures? Am I trying to escape working at my relationship and making it more interesting? Is it really that my psychological hang-ups, economic problems, career difficulties, are bothering me, and the affair is a diversion from the painful task of solving these problems? Is my dissatisfaction with my relationship part of my general negative feeling about myself rather than a true reflection of my relationship?

If I am feeling sexually deprived, have I given my mate the right of 'first refusal,' that is, what have I done recently to increase sexual pleasure with my spouse? Was it a persistent, honest effort? Am I actually that deprived sexually or am I using that as a rationalization to have a 'justified' affair? Do I merely *want* variety or am I insisting that I absolutely *need* it, *must* have it?"

An individual can ask him- or herself questions like these, or a couple may engage in a dialogue based on these questions in an effort to determine what is wrong, if anything, and what a workable solution might be. Of course, an immediate, insightful answer will not always be forthcoming. An individual or a couple may well come up with few, if any, clear answers, or "answers" may be discovered that later prove to be false. Honest scrutiny of motives is not a foolproof course. It is difficult to be sure whether one's inquiries are logical or self-deceptive, or to predict with complete accuracy the effects of one's actions. But when your relationship, your well-being, or your spouse's well-being is at stake, this questioning process can be critical and instructive. Indeed, it can be the beginning of a new beginning.

Sound Thinking and Smart Moves

1. Anyone who considers an affair in an effort to complete themselves has probably been watching too many romance movies, or reading the same. Love is wonderful, new love is especially wonderful, but we are each responsible for our own completion. Intimate relationships are an important part of personal growth, but while they play a part in growing emotionally healthy, the effort requires both parties to participate fully.

2. The prospect of an affair, or one already in place creates a feeling of excitement. It's definitely an uplifting feeling, but embedded in that feeling is a danger signal that is often ignored. That is unfortunate because it contains a life-altering warning should the affair be discovered, and even if not discovered an affair is not without effect on a primary relationship.

3. While the question, "Why?" is sure to be asked when an affair is discovered, the response is likely to be unsettling since it is often stated in a manner that leaves the uninvolved partner feeling like it was his or her fault. Before the affair-involved responds to "Why?," it is wise to think it through and put the response forward in a manner that does not blame the uninvolved partner. For example, "I couldn't make myself happy" is preferable to "You didn't meet my needs."

Chapter 4

DISCOVERY: AN EMOTIONAL CRISIS

ACCIDENTAL DETECTION?

Reactions to the discovery of an extra-relationship affair can include a vast array of emotions such as rage, pain, jealousy, confusion, and grief (Peluso & Spina, 2008). A common reaction to discovering an extra-relationship affair is the shattered trust that results in continuously looking for additional or ongoing signs of betrayal, a condition of hypervigilance; a global feeling characterized by suspicion and difficulty trusting others (Gordon et al., 2004; Fife et al., 2008b). As suggested by the American Association for Marriage and Family Therapy (2013), daily activities can become impaired and concentration can be challenged due to constant thoughts about the affair and the sting of a shattered trust. While all breaches are traumatic, the most traumatized noninvolved partners tend to be those who possessed the greatest trust and were least suspecting of an extra-relationship affair. One woman's experience illustrates the trauma that commonly occurs:

"I was going to a male psychologist at the time and I remember telling him I thought my husband was seeing other women. He kept asking me why I was so untrusting and insecure. He confused me and my husband confused me. Yet I was right after all. My instincts weren't wrong. I found out through my husband's phone that he *was* having affairs. He left a tell-tale text on it. He was also seen with her at a restaurant we have eaten at as well. I was appalled. I begged him to stop. I carried on. I screamed, 'If you loved me, you wouldn't do this!' I ranted and raved and thought I was going to have a nervous break-down. It took a long time for me to calm down. I felt like killing him, and at one point, I even got up to get a kitchen knife. I was frightened; frightened I might turn it on myself, my depression was raging.

"During the course of the night, he made a clean breast of a whole lot of things he'd been doing over the past years; different women, women in his office, old friends of ours, business arrangements, and that sort of thing. He said none of it had been important to him; no one person. And he swore he'd change, give it all up. I believed him, it sounded as if he were honest. I assumed my crying and misery had had an impact on him. He was very apologetic and during the next year he kept bringing home gifts for me, and he was generally more thoughtful than he'd ever been. I was flattered, reassured, and I began to relax. Then there was this night when we were driving by his office after a movie, and he suggested we go up and screw on the rug. I found that very sexy. It was a Saturday night, the building was dark and empty; I felt as if this was a clandestine kind of thing and was very excited. I really got into a whole fantasy about it. After we made love and had gotten dressed, he went into the bathroom. He was taking a really long time, and I was sitting behind his desk waiting for him. After a while, I opened a drawer and staring me in the face was a letter that started out, 'To my lover.'"

"Just then I heard him come out of the bathroom, and I grabbed the let-ter and put it in my pocket. When he came over to embrace me, I maneu-vered around him saying I had to go now: 'It must have been something we ate.' In the bathroom, I read the letter. I was shocked. The letter was from a woman he worked with. It was a love letter. She described her feelings about an evening they had spent together the previous week. I remember that night. I wanted his companionship; I felt lonely. He told me he had a dinner date with a potentially important customer from out of town. 'It's one of those things,' he had said. The bastard! The letter mentioned me. This woman said she was jealous of me; she couldn't stand separating from him. She wanted him all for herself. She described some very private moments they shared. I felt as if someone had cut me open and pulled out my insides, my depression was profound. Never have I felt so exposed, so vulnerable, betrayed. I trusted him; he had promised to stop a year ago when I was so distressed, but even then he wasn't honest. I threw up. After a while, I came out of the bathroom, and although I was shivering all night as if I were in shock, I didn't let on I knew anything. I could not tolerate another lie while we faced each other eye-to-eye."

****

As the research and clinical experience indicate, when one partner discovers that a spouse is having an affair, the reaction is often profound shock followed by hurt, anger, and sometimes even guilt. It appears at times that the discovery is not always accidental. The woman describing her experiences above detected infidelity twice. A diary kept, letters not destroyed, a phone record not deleted, an Internet trail still available, sometimes an indiscreet choice of meeting places, do these have a deliberate element?

Obviously, keeping extra-relationship sexual activities a total secret from one's mate takes some work. Besides the various possibilities of disclosure noted earlier, there are innumerable others—an automobile accident; being seen by a friend; a chance encounter by a relative; an unpredicted change in plans by a mate, and venereal disease, which can be very difficult to explain if one's uninvolved mate is afflicted. This is to say nothing of changes in attitude and behavior at home that arouse a mate's suspicions. In addition, there are telltale signs of extra-relationship sexual enthusiasm—smudged lipstick, unfamiliar perfume traces, bites, bruises, and scratches garnered in the heat of passion. Sometimes the evidence is deliberately planted by a lover to make trouble at home and force a separation.

Neither is it unknown for the affair-involved to summon a mate's attention by deliberately flaunting the affair, or at least a serious flirtation. Mental health practitioners are quite familiar with the husband or wife who is so careless with incriminating evidence that "accidental" detection is virtually inevitable. Such behavior may be a way of forcing the hand of a mate who refused to acknowledge that a relationship is in trouble. Detection may also serve the purpose of partners who want their mates to dissolve the relationship, thereby relieving them of guilt and enabling them to plead "circumstances" (or at least "I should be forgiven") to children, relatives, and friends.

Thus, in an empty relationship, a mate may flaunt infidelity to provoke a spouse to divorce. Where the partnership is merely troubled, an affair may be a signal to the indifferent partner to pay more attention to the relationship. Of course, most people do not willingly acknowledge that the brazenness of their extrarelationship involvements conveys such purposes. Nor does the effect intended usually become the effect achieved. The husband who is indiscreetly conducting an affair to force his wife to pay more attention to him may find that she has been disgusted with the relationship for some time and this brazenness has merely provided the opportunity she has been waiting for to file for a divorce. Or a wife who is trying to provoke a husband into walking out on her may find herself trapped when her husband uses the detected affair as emotional and financial blackmail, threatens to disclose her behavior to the children and her parents, thereby exacting a pound of flesh.

While some affairs, initiated by a man or a woman may be strategic to get the other person's attention, the majority have no such motive, and if discovered are interpersonally, and intrapersonally disastrous and the basis for depression. This is particularly true for women who find their mate to be extra-relationship involved, although depression is also a frequent symptom for men who are betrayed as well (Hall & Fincham, 2005 O'Leary, 2005). There are three major negative events in a primary relationship that are likely to result in clinical depression of women within one month of the event. These events include physical aggression against her, threatening to leave her, and discovering an extra-relationship affair (Cano & O'Leary, 2000; O'Leary, 2005). For women without a history of depression, the probability of becoming depressed after discovering an extramarital affair was found to be 38 percent.

For women with previous history of depression, their vulnerability is increased and the likelihood of becoming depressed again after learning of infidelity was 72 percent (Cano & O'Leary, 2000). In fact, according to Cano and O'Leary's research, women were more likely to become depressed after discovering infidelity than after being the victim of moderate physical aggression such as pushing, slapping, or shoving.

NO, THIS ISN'T HAPPENING

Denial, another factor common to discovery however, does not appear to discriminate, both genders would rather not believe that the life they thought they had is not the life they have. An individual will deny a mate's obvious extra-relationship sexual involvement because acknowledgment may be so threatening that it cannot be tolerated. Arthur Fay, a large man with imposing stature, is a biologist in his early forties who specializes in cancer research. Fay is not the type of man easily forgotten. His direct, assertive manner leaves an impression on most people; they either appreciate him dearly or feel threatened and intimidated. His wife Beth also makes a notable impression. She is fair-skinned with shiny red hair, busty, and long-legged. Though not as gregarious as her husband, she makes up for it with her striking looks and quiet, keen intellect.

Mr. and Mrs. Fay sought professional help with their relationship for "communication difficulties." Frequently, this is a catchall statement that masks more specific dissatisfactions. In the sessions, it turned out that Mr. Fay wanted his wife to be more affectionate and sexual with him. Mrs. Fay wanted him to stop making so much of an issue about sex: "You know I am not a naturally affectionate person!" Mr. Fay complained frequently that his wife spent too much time away from home, and worse yet, as soon as she came in from an evening's volunteer work, would announce she had a headache, felt severely fatigued, or give some other excuse that would preclude sexual intimacy. Complaints, countercomplaints, and dissatisfaction were longstanding in the marriage. In the year before seeking professional intervention, Mr. Fay felt particularly sexually deprived and resentful. Partway into their first therapy session together, the following dialogue took place:

Beth Fay:	And another thing, you seem to resent my going out at night. The charity organizations I work for depend on me and that's important to me. All you worry about is how you can get in touch with me. I keep telling you the hospital Internet connection is terrible, at least it is in the sections I am in. I don't hear your calls.
Therapist:	Beth, you seem to be implying that your husband doesn't trust you. Is that so?
Beth Fay:	(beginning to blush) Yes, either that or he is trying to control me and resents my independence.
Therapist:	In what way might he not trust you?
Beth Fay:	(neck and face turning crimson red) I don't know; you'll have to ask him.
Arthur Fay:	(sitting stiffly and staring away from his wife's obvious emotional reaction to the therapist's probe) I'm not trying to control my wife; I would just like to see more of her.

At this point, the therapist did not pursue the possibility of affair involvement any further and at the end of the hour arranged to see Mr. and Mrs. Fay the following week, but Mrs. Fay showed up without her husband and pleaded to talk, rather than come in the following week with her husband who was called out-of-town. The therapist reluctantly agreed and Mrs. Fay acknowledged an affair that had been going on for little over a year. Mr. Fay, a bright, scientifically trained, socially aware man, had come practically face-to-face with his wife's adultery, but he had blinded himself to the evidence. This is obviously an area where clinical experience, rather than empirical research is going to be more telling, and clinical experience suggests Mr. Fay's denial is not an isolated case. In other instances where a man or woman is not prepared to see and experience a traumatic and life-changing incident, they simply or not so simply color it, distort it, or ignore it

TRUE CONFESSIONS

There are times when an affair does not require accidental discovery to be discovered. A suspicious relationship partner may hire a detective to gather definitive evidence, or put a tracker on his vehicle, spyware on a computer, or perhaps use the phone to track whereabouts. These tactics are sometimes employed at the urging of a lawyer, or maybe a friend, and even then with great reluctance because of its humiliating effects on both relationship partners. More commonly, some adulterous people feel compelled to confess their sexual misadventures to their mate. The motives behind voluntary confessions lacking suspicion vary; guilt and the need to be forgiven are common.

A typical pattern following an abrupt confession to one's spouse is that the one who confesses becomes the target of anger, hostility, and shame. He or she may then experience punishment, and as a result, feel cleansed and restored to innocence:

"I had this nagging guilt. My wife and I are close; we share things together and have a commitment to each other. My deception about the affair really bothered me. There were a number of underhanded things I noticed myself doing to ease my discomfort. For example, I would come home and be very critical, provoke fights, in fact. What I really wanted was for Joyce to say, 'You son of a bitch, go to hell!' Something that would relieve me of my responsibility. This way I could say to myself, 'Well, we're on the outs; the old rules are null and void.' The problem is that Joyce is so tolerant of me that it didn't work. I couldn't get her to give up on me. I also tried flirting in front of her, hoping that she would take the hint and give me permission, like, 'Oh, I can see you want to make it with another woman, go ahead, be my guest.' That didn't work either, she wasn't about to offer her best wishes—that tolerant she wasn't. After a while, being too damned honest and conscientious for my own good, I couldn't keep things secret from her.

"It happened like this: We were at a party and Susan Fields was there. I said to my wife, 'I want to leave, let's get out of here; there is something I have to talk to you about.' She said, 'What's wrong?' and I told her that we'd discuss it on the way home. As we drove away from the party, I told her about my affair with Susan. It was a mistake; I knew it as soon as I started because her face flushed in a real scary sort of way, but it was too late. Her voice cracked as she asked me a lot of questions. Then she sort of curled up within herself and suffered in silence. If she had fought me, it might have turned me against her, and I could deal with that. But she was so hurt and so deeply unhappy, I couldn't handle it. Neither could she. We survived, but it left quite a scar on both of us."

When suspicion and mistrust arising out of extra-relationship involvement is a serious barrier to intimacy and the deceived partner continues to probe the issue, minimally a frank discussion, preferably with the assistance of a therapist, may be a start to improving the relationship. Of course, even at this juncture some people may choose not to be candid. A person remaining with a partner for expediency's sake, for instance, a mother with several children who stays with her husband because she has no hope of employment, and who wants nothing from the relationship except financial support, may continue to lie in an effort to maintain the relationship. But those who wish to improve their relationship and foster mutual growth and trust would best consider honesty if the relationship is troubled by an underlying mistrust.

In cases such as the one detailed above, where there is little or no suspicion on the part of the mate, clinicians experienced with treating couples may feel there is a good chance "enlightenment" will serve no constructive purpose and may well be severely disturbing to the unsuspecting. As a consequence, the confessor not only doesn't experience the return to innocence sought but frequently feels more like a heel. Further, the need to confess more often than not is a self-serving act to relieve guilt cloaked in a rationalization to renegotiate or remodel the relationship contract. Confirmatory views of the lack of wisdom of this type of behavior are found among some of the leading professionals specializing in the marital/primary relationship. Carlfred B. Broderick (1970), formerly the director of the marriage and family counselor training program at the University of Southern California, offers his opinion in the journal *Medical Aspects of Human Sexuality*:

> Like any other remedy, confession of extra-relationship affairs to a spouse is only helpful under certain conditions. I have cases where such a confession set couples therapy back several weeks and at least two instances where it disrupted the marriage completely. Indeed, the potential for damage is so real that I have become a conservative on this issue. . . . There is no simple rule of thumb that can govern all cases, but experience indicates that a conservative attitude toward confession is well justified.

Dr. Harold Winn (1970), clinical professor of psychiatry at Temple University Medical Center, writing in the same journal, asks the question: "Should a husband or wife confess infidelity?" and answers: "In general, the response to this question is No." Dr. Winn points out that a confession of this sort may possibly relieve the guilt of the adulterer but frequently will not be taken well by the other partner, and may actually be an act of conscious or unconscious hostility toward this partner. Also, writing in the same journal, Dr. Charles E. Llewellyn (1970), professor of psychiatry at Duke University Medical Center, adds his view:

> Should a husband or wife confess infidelity? An informal poll of friends, secretaries, colleagues, and students yielded a unanimous "No," but many elaborated their answers. I agree with the general statement, "No." . . . In my opinion a husband or wife should not confess infidelity to the other unless he or she feels it necessary. I recommend that the involved partner discuss the situation with someone who is qualified to understand and work with the complexities of the situation and its meaning to the potential confessor, to the spouse, and to the marriage.

Even a high-ranking clergyman agreed. Bishop James Pike (1967) wrote that when two lovers have decided an affair is justifiable, they may have an obligation to lie about it for the good of the others: "Once a primary ethical decision has been made a particular way, more often than not secondary ethical responsibilities (i.e., secrecy and deception) are entailed."

Is all this to say that honesty that is both direct and full between husband and wife had best be thrown to the wind? No, this is not the point. It is simply that most of us, in response to, "Did you have a nice day, dear?" are not ready for, "Oh yes, I spent the morning at a business meeting and spent the afternoon with a terrific lover, screwing to my heart's content. And how was your day, dear?" When a mate is unsuspecting, and the affair is in the past, discretion, consideration, tact, and sensitive selectivity are suggested.

Following this suggestion leads to one of the limitations of an affair: the joy of it does not lend itself to sharing with one's spouse. This is a limitation, but unless the affair is so time-consuming or suspicion-generating that cover-up lying becomes the rule rather than the exception, some clinicians believe it does not necessarily limit relationship intimacy (Ellis, 2003). Real intimacy does not mean full disclosure of one's thoughts, feelings, and actions, they suggest. Real intimacy is experienced only when people have the capacity and wisdom to give and to withhold, to move toward and to move away from, to be close and to be distant. In the great majority of relationships, total openness and closeness are oppressive and smothering goals, they maintain. When the issue is extra-relationship involvement, a "true confession" other than when it is pressing, as it is in the case of ongoing suspicion, full disclosure is especially likely to produce panic and pain rather than permanence and peace.

PANIC AND PAIN

The desire to be special to someone, to be "number one," to be wanted above all others, probably burns in all of us. No matter that this is an unrealistic ideal; the ground rules of traditional primary relationships attempt to secure it by emphasizing sexual exclusivity. The conventional clandestine affair to most of us constitutes a breach of trust, a violation of the implicitly agreed-upon rules. When the deception is discovered, as we have seen, emotions ranging from panic to furious rage frequently result. Behavior varies and ranges from the passivity of depression to violence.

True, there may be people who are so secure that they are not strongly threatened by the discovery of their spouse's affair and who react with tolerance, understanding, and calmness. But, as Gracie Allen used to say, "There are a lot of people like that, but not many." Even those who have been having secret liaisons of their own react with deep shock, anger, and jealousy when they discover that their partner has been doing the same. Some people, so hurt by the experience, will view it as unforgivable and will move to break up the relationship, usually a relationship that wasn't highly regarded. Others will see it as a symptom of what has been lacking in their relationship and will set out to do something about it. Still others will view it as not symptomatic of anything in particular and work toward a mutual agreement about such behavior.

And there are those who will "stick it out" for reasons of economics, insecurity, children, or whatever, but will likely have a side-by-side, rather than a face-to-face relationship.

Sometimes the discovery of an affair merely heightens a conflict, such as a lack of affection between partners because of the emotion and time being drawn from the relationship. This is most likely to occur if either the affair or the relationship is highly involved. Of course, it is possible that more, rather than less, emotion will flow into the relationship as a result of an affair, but the effect is more often one of deprivation and conflict.

Where the extra-relationship sexual involvement is casual and the primary relationship is low involvement, the effect on the relationship may be very small until the affair is discovered. Then it is primarily the knowledge of the affair rather than the affair per se that is disruptive. A standard line of dialogue in Hollywood movies and novels used to involve a husband or wife discovering that the spouse has been unfaithful. "I suppose you'll want a divorce," one of them says, implying that divorce is the inevitable outcome of detected infidelity. This is indeed true in some relationships, but divorce is less frequently sought because of infidelity alone. An affair that is dramatically discovered may be the final indignity that shatters a troubled relationship, but when two persons have gotten along together reasonably well, one episode of infidelity will be less likely to trigger a divorce action. It may produce shock and resentment, and sometimes even physical estrangement, but not a sudden divorce. When adultery's ultimate impact on a long-term relationship is divorce, it is usually the last straw in a slow, prolonged process of deterioration. Or, it is an affair that is so damaging—for example, an involvement with a partner's best friend or sibling—that it shatters even a reasonably close relationship.

COPING: DESTRUCTIVE TACTICS

With respect to the ultimate effect of a discovered affair, an important consideration is the affair-involved motivation, whether this is a fling primarily, or on the other end of the spectrum, an exit move. Of course, another consideration depends, critically, on the spouse's interpretation of what the affair means and how well the spouse is able to manage the considerable wound to trust and stability.

Sometimes it goes something like, "My partner is having extramarital relations because I am not loved anymore and my partner cannot bear to have me around because I am either stupid, boring, annoying, insensitive, incompetent, or all of the above. Furthermore, I am sexually inadequate. This relationship is going to end our marriage! OMG, what will others think if they find out about this?" Obviously, partners who believe that an affair means they are no longer loved; or that it is indicative of their own worthlessness, or their worthlessness in their partner's eyes will feel and act differently from those who do not conclude from the experience that they are inadequate and their relationship is hopeless.

Most of us have inflated sexual behavior to unrealistic proportions. For one thing, we equate sex with intimacy. This is true sometimes but certainly not always; sex is frequently not intimate, and intimacy often does not include sex. Moreover, infidelity, loosely defined as a breach of trust, may occur in many nonsexual aspects of a relationship but it is primarily the sexual or deep emotional tie that distresses us.

This leads to some interesting reactions; a person may be destroyed by a spouse's extra-relationship sexuality, even if assured it was casual and non-intimate, others may be disturbed by a sexual fling, but floored by a mate's involvement with another in an intimate nonsexual exchange. The point here is that extra-relationship involvement, like all behavior, is open to many interpretations and the particular interpretation chosen is crucial to the feelings that are generated. Consequently, a man or woman who becomes distraught on learning of a mate's affair has several choices in expressing that feeling. She can, for example, proceed to suffer in grand and glorious style, all the while hoping that her mate will notice her pain and prove his love by rejecting the outside relationship:

Mate One:	(letting her lip tremble just so) If you don't stop running around, we might as well get a divorce.
Mate Two:	(in frustrated anger) Don't be silly. You don't really want a divorce!
Mate One:	I do! Don't you care about our marriage and what I'll have to go through being single again?
Mate Two:	(feeling guilty) Of course I care! What kind of a person do you think I am? I do a lot of things for you!
Mate One:	You're selfish. You only do things that you care about. If you really cared about our marriage, you wouldn't have Sally Andrews on your to-do list. It's your fault that I'm eating too much and getting fat. I do it out of the frustration you cause. You're going to drive me to suicide!

This approach is characteristic of the wronged mate who is passive and timid. The hurt is turned inward and is expressed in the form of an accident, neglect of health, suicide attempts, and other self-destructive behavior. In the type of communication just illustrated, emotional distress is used as a tool to manipulate the involved mate. The object here is not direct and honest expression of authentic feelings; it is to induce guilt in the involved spouse and thereby control his behavior. The message is: "Stop what you are doing or I shall be even more miserable. You, not I, am in charge of my emotions."

This attempt to control a partner through guilt is often accompanied by an appeal to duty: "You owe it to me to stop seeing her." The pairing of a self-pitying moralist such as this and a guilt-prone adulterer provides an ideal setup for a destructive interaction. The moralist can play prosecutor, judge, and jury on one occasion, and then, in his additional role as victim, feel rejected, and sorry for himself or herself, all the while provoking a guilty squirm or a flurry of angry self-defense mumbles from the affair-involved spouse. But this ploy has its disadvantages. As Bertrand Russell (1933) has written, "In former days parents ruined their relations with children by preaching love as a duty; husbands and wives still too often ruin their relations to each other by the same mistake. Love cannot be a duty because it is not subject to the will."

Replaying the guilt/obligation/duty message often enough frequently does exert a strong influence. Even if the unfaithful spouse is a low-guilt type, it plays upon his dislike of disruption at home and fear of being disgraced if his indiscretions become publicized. The impact is so potent that it sometimes terminates the relationship along with the affair, especially if the affair-involved makes his partner's acting-out all about his well-being. Consider:

"My wife and I had what I could call a guarded relationship. There were several touchy areas that we both avoided. When she found out about my other involvements, she initially used an appeal to sympathy—tears, outcries, visible suffering; then she resorted to what she called 'a reduction of services'—cold dinners, uncooperativeness, and the like; and then the final blow, an overdose of sleeping pills. One night, I came home late from a business meeting—I had stopped seeing other women months before—and she was lying unconscious in the middle of the living-room floor. There was an empty bottle of sleeping pills nearby where I couldn't miss them. I called the police and we took her to the emergency room where her stomach was pumped. She stayed overnight at the hospital and was released the following afternoon. That was it. The last straw; I couldn't take it anymore. I felt like a complete heel all over again. Suppose I hadn't come home when I did and she had succeeded? How could I live with that? How could I leave the house every day not knowing what she would do? I was frantic. How could I face anyone who found out what this was all about? For the first time in months, I started to consider leaving again. I just couldn't take the pressure anymore."

Occasionally, a spouse whose mate is unfaithful will make a desperate effort to "get his act together." A man may lose weight, become more discerning about his dress and general appearance, and be extremely attentive to his wife in an effort to compete with the third party. Following the suggestions of many women's magazines, a woman will make a concerted effort to be seductive, sexy, and passionate. But anger, hurt, and jealousy are hardly conducive to such behavior. The "act" denies that there is a healing process that can and usually does take some time as the experience of Dori and Alvin indicates.

Dori and Alvin are in their early forties. Two weeks before Dori discovered that Alvin was having an affair, and since then, despite his discontinuance of the affair, she has been trying to deny her distress. Her attempts to play up to Alvin are both an effort to keep him and an attempt to distract from her emotional pain. They have just finished having intercourse. She has pretended passion, but she is not a good actress:

Alvin: You don't seem to be getting much out of this anymore.

Dori: Oh no, I enjoy it.

Alvin: You don't seem to enjoy it like you used to.

Dori: (her bitterness getting the best of her) You're not like you used to be.

Alvin: (feeling angry) What the hell does that mean?

Dori: Oh, Alvin, forget it. In a while, things will be better again. Let's give it some time.

Alvin: (his guilt and anger rising) I suppose you're referring to that thing with Florence Jackson.

Dori: I don't want to talk about that!

Alvin: Look, these things happen. Nobody's perfect!

Dori: All right, then, I'm not perfect either. Let's forget it.

Alvin: Forget it, my ass. You won't let me forget, that's clear from the cold shoulder you've been giving me in bed.

Dori: I never turn you down.

Alvin: But you never turn me on either. You go through the motions, but it's empty.

Dori: Alvin, don't push me. I'm doing all I can.

Alvin: (still feeling provoked and guilty) Do you think I like making love to a woman who's cold? This must be your way of getting back!

Dori: I'm not getting back at you. I'm trying to forget it! It's just that I have trouble feeling the same way I used to. Maybe in time it will get better. Time heals all wounds.

Alvin: If you want to call it quits, just let me know.

Dori: (her suppressed anger surfacing) So you can get back together with your girlfriend!

Alvin: Oh, for cryin' out loud, I've told you. . .

And so on. While angry outbursts and counter-outbursts are very common, this kind of communication characterizes two people who underestimate the effect the discovery of an affair has had. Alvin is insisting Dori be "normal" so that he doesn't feel guilty, and Dori disregards her emotional pain to keep the peace and to keep Alvin. The important feelings, underlying attitudes, and concerns go untouched. If denial and avoidance were not so prominent, this couple might have started a dialogue to examine their feelings toward each other and perhaps get on a path to healing. In a later chapter we will see Dori and Alvin interacting after further treatment.

Sometimes a hurt, distressed mate tries retaliation. If John develops a sexual involvement with Helen, a friend of his wife Mary, then Mary may begin to go to bed with all of John's friends, and after doing so, throw it in his face. The result of this contest to see who can have the most extra-relationship sex and hurt the other most brutally is usually an empty relationship and empty sex. Consider:

"I was so hurt and angered by the discovery of my husband's affair that I did nothing for four days but cry. My face was puffy and raw. I couldn't hold food; my weight fell well below normal. After those initial days, I refer to them now as days of mourning; I started to plot and scheme. I tried to think of the best way of getting back. Howard has a brother. He is two years younger; he and Howard have been competitive all their lives. I know his brother finds me attractive. He's even made passes at me. I decided to seduce him. It worked without a hitch; his brother was most cooperative. Of course, when Howard found out, which I knew he would, he felt as if someone had driven a truck through his stomach. He came home infuriated, but he managed to keep his cool. I immediately knew what was up and I walked into our older daughter's bedroom with her and closed the door. He came charging in and said to her, 'Do you know what your mother did?' She replied, 'Yes, she told me, and I'm glad because you're a son of a bitch, and if that made her feel better, you deserve it!' That did it. He exploded; he was enraged. He pulled one of the wooden posts right off her bed and began smashing things. The room looked as if a bomb had exploded in it. I ran to call the police and he ripped the phone off the wall. He went insane. It was only then that I could stand back and feel compassion."

In other instances, the previously faithful partner may not flaunt the newly anointed affair in his or her mate's face. Merely knowing that "justice is being served" brings temporary relief but certainly not healing. In other cases, the avenger subtly humiliates his spouse by conducting his illicit sex in such a way that the mate's friends and work associates know and the mate finds out through them. This is what occurred in the aforementioned instance. Still others disclose their retaliation by evidence left about the house or scream it out in dramatic and frequently violent scenes. None of these actions is productive; sometimes they even have tragic consequences. One man who had been extra-relationship involved, when confronted with his wife's retaliation, committed suicide.

In another case, a young secretary, who little suspected that she was merely a weapon in a marital war, killed herself when the affair was abruptly terminated.

Without guidance and with pain running wild each conversation ends in a disruption; there is a lack of honest expression of feelings. Trust is not restored by these bouts and the fighting is likely to continue until the relationship is torn apart or has seriously deteriorated. Since these encounters are so sensitive, the communication is likely to be nonproductive. Once emotions are directed toward the honest expression of feelings, it is important to examine what happened and its implications. What factors in the relationship system that the couple formed have bearing on the affair? Was the affair part of a larger pattern of distrust and deception in the relationship? Are there things that can be done differently and more effectively in the relationship? What are the hopes and expectations for the future?

Very specifically, what kinds of behavior are acceptable and what kinds out of bounds? Some couples may wish to renegotiate and remodel their relationship agreement without restricting themselves to traditional sex-role expectations and definitions of fidelity. Others may resolve upon conventional standards. Still others, and this may involve a large number, may continue to differ bitterly and require professional intervention.

If it was a high-involvement affair, the noninvolved mate has a right to know where he or she stands and rarely can be reassured quickly or easily. A shattered emotional investment of five, ten, twenty, or more years' duration is not easily repaired. It may be months or years before trust and a sense of security are reestablished. The relationship may never be the same. It is not unusual for the aggrieved spouse secretly to open up a separate bank account and take other actions to be financially protected in case of a recurrence or the dissolution of the relationship. This protective behavior may continue despite what looks like the beginning of a healing on the surface.

ATTACHMENT WOUNDS

Sometimes discussion of touchy issues can disrupt a relationship further by reopening old wounds and heightening distress to intolerable levels. If this occurs, it is time to work with a person in one of the psychological professions. Therapy may help pace interaction at a manageable rate and guide it along constructive lines. Even therapy, however, will only work if both mates want it, if both will start to listen as well as talk, and if both partners will confront therapy issues openly rather than retreat into wounded silence or endless angry eruptions.

While all effort may be made to repair a relationship after discovery of an affair, the discovery can sometimes have devastating and lasting impact on the betrayed partner (Gordon & Baucom, 2003). The discovery of an extramarital affair may lead to uncertainty, link to past losses, and deep and lasting pain (Fife et al., 2008a). The betrayed partner will often feel intense emotions of shame, depression, powerlessness, and abandonment. Feelings of rage, shock, numbness, and denial are common. This result from the betrayal can develop into "attachment injury." Attachment injury stems from betrayal resulting in abandonment and/or damage of trust in the relationship (Winek & Craven, 2003).

Indeed, when an adulterous mate acts to restore the relationship and the spouse continues to grieve for a long time, there may be old emotional injuries that have been activated and connected to the current emotional wound. He or she may be reacting to childhood hurts, such as his or her parent's divorce, or a father who neglected his family for his work, or a mother who had no time to show love for her children or was abandoned by a husband, or an old adolescent wound may have been reopened, and the distressed spouse may be reacting as occurred earlier in life.

A developmental task of childhood involves moving beyond dependency on the parent. A similar process must be repeated in the intimate partnerships of adulthood. If it is not, the discovery of an affair will be followed by unbearable and unceasing distress. In these instances, therapy is indicated. The best antidote to persistent distress is growth toward autonomy and self-direction. This kind of personal strength can make healing less painful. A discovered adultery does not have to be a disaster; it is a traumatic experience but like practically all emotional experiences, presents an opportunity for movement toward growth.

Sound Thinking and Smart Moves

1. There are occasions when a woman is filled with suspicion as to her partner's lack of fidelity. We saw this in the woman describing her experience to a psychologist who strongly questioned her suspicions. She was correct; her husband had been affair-involved. Clinical experience suggests that she has plenty of company with her suspicions—when a woman is suspicious there is often something to be suspicious about. Her partner's denial despite her strong and persistent suspicion is bound to make things worse.

2. Confession comes in two forms—voluntary and "you're busted!" In both instances, a confession that leaves out important factors ("Okay, so there were two women.") is going to damage the healing process of the noninvolved partner. If more is discovered, and it often is, the emotional wound is poked and reinjured. Truth can be frightening but if trust is to be restored it is critical. Sometimes discussion for some people is best completed in scheduled meetings with each other—the most difficult issues discussed first and graphic images—the kind that will haunt the noninvolved partner—left out.

3. Dr. Carl Jung, many years ago was quoted as saying, "What you resist persists." His wisdom would wisely be applied to the grieving process the noninvolved mate experiences. Grief is the normal psychological, social, and physical reaction to a loss. It is experienced through our feelings, thoughts, and our behavior with others. It is not something to be ashamed of, or to apologize for; allowing oneself to own the experience without apology facilitates healing, denial does not.

Chapter 5

POSITIVE EFFECTS

AGAINST THE ODDS

Extra-relationship sex in our society is fraught with difficulties, dangers, and risks. The time commitment, emotional investment, deception, and lying, as well as the decreased attention and affection to one's spouse that may occur, most frequently lead to several negative effects. These include at least: (1) an erosion of communication, trust, and security; (2) the stimulation of destructive jealousy and the heightening of feelings of inadequacy; and (3) the rapid and agonizing deterioration of a shaky and only intermittently satisfactory relationship should the affair be discovered; (4) children are likely to be emotionally neglected, whether the affair is undiscovered, but stealing a parent's attention, or discovered and impacting them through their parent's discord; (5) the family household is likely to be divided, impacting all family members emotionally, and sometimes financially as well. Indeed, even solid, well-functioning relationships are likely to be rocked and seriously damaged by an outside amorous involvement.

The damage may be sharp and sudden when provoked by discovery, or slow and subtle when the affair is undiscovered but long-term, draining the energy from the primary relationship. Aside from being detrimental to the emotional well-being of one's mate and family, affairs conflict with middle-class mores and can be professionally and socially hazardous. The instances in which extra-relationship sex is handled carelessly and neurotically are legion. The results are messy, emotionally painful, and disruptive. Broken families and broken people are not an uncommon consequence.

The Judeo-Christian tradition, which has always been critical of the enticements and rewards of adultery, deems the act nothing more than an indulgence of animalistic instinct by people who are emotionally weak and spiritually empty. This is one view of adultery.

The other part of the story is that extra-relationship sex can in some instances have positive effects on maturity, personal growth, and the primary relationship. Families are not impacted by events, such as infidelity, in the same way. Infidelity can result in conflict, divorce, but bring some couples closer (Reibstein & Burbach, 2013). Responsible and irresponsible, well-coupled and poorly coupled, happy and unhappy people are sexually monogamous. The same applies to non-monogamous arrangements. Many work well and some of those that are borderline or unstable, manage to survive and benefit the participants. While research in this area is scant, clinical experience suggests the same applies to extra-relationship arrangements.

Julia, a thirty-three-year-old high school English teacher, has been married six years and has a three-year-old son. Her husband, Bruce, is an architect. Julia has a warm, pleasant face and her eyes sparkle as she talks about her affair:

"I have known Fred for four years; his wife and I work together. During the times we have been together, at parties, school functions, and so on, Fred would usually flirt with me. Since I noticed that he flirted with many of the other women, I never thought much of it. Then two years ago he started to call me and ask me out. He's a salesman and arranges his own hours. At this point, I still didn't take him seriously, or didn't want to, and jokingly put him off. I would say things like, 'You must have the wrong number' or 'What's a nice guy like you. . .?' When I look back, the way I denied my feelings about those initial flirtations, and later, the more direct invitations, was so typical of me. My feelings so often get buried under words. It's an occupational hazard. I still have a strong tendency to talk about my feelings rather than experiencing them, but less so now. Fred persisted and eventually I relented. Strange how it happened. I called him. One day I was in his neighborhood—with no real reason to be there—and I decided to see if he was home. He was, and we met in a bar. From the moment we sat facing each other alone, on a cloudy, gloomy afternoon in that bar, it felt good to me. It felt right.

"We drank and we talked, and talked and drank, until we were both very high and had told each other an awful lot about ourselves. That's how we spent the first afternoon together. The next time we met, a week later in the early evening, we were both starving so we drove over to a delightful out-of-the-way restaurant and picked up right where we left off, talking. We talked all the way through dinner and into the evening. He told me about his marriage and I told him about mine. He gave me the idea that his wasn't the greatest and he stayed away evenings for that reason, but he didn't pretend for a minute that he was considering divorce.

"We continued to meet and talk. First there was a good-night kiss, then petting. After about three months, we had intercourse. Our sexual relationship was fantastic. I had never been as sexually excited and responsive as I was with Fred. But this wasn't the important thing; most important to me was the whole way I felt about myself when I was with Fred. This is when I first became aware of how distant I am from my feelings. Fred confronted me constantly. In a compassionate and loving way, he prodded me to express my feelings, to act on them, to be alive! We did such outrageous things together, I was really beginning to be less controlled; I was trusting myself more, trusting my instincts. I realized then that Bruce, as sweet as he is, is also out of touch with his feelings. We were both on a treadmill racing to keep up with the Joneses, the American dream, big house, two cars, prestige, achievement, everything that, in the final analysis, is of no consequence. I panicked when I first realized that. 'Would I be able to continue with my marriage now? Would it be too stifling? Could Bruce also grow or had I outgrown him?' These questions plagued me. I didn't want to break up my marriage, but what I was experiencing was too important to ignore. I had done enough of that!

"It is very difficult to be reborn, and I didn't want to return to the deadness. This is where the panic came in. I knew there was no returning. I wouldn't allow myself to vegetate as I had been doing all my life, at any cost. Either Bruce came along on the trip or I was determined to take it alone. It occurred to me that Bruce could also benefit from an affair. I fantasized some woman opening his eyes to life the way Fred had done for me. This could potentially enrich our relationship, but I never pursued it beyond fantasy. It was too risky, and I didn't have the guts to suggest it. My first impulse with Bruce was to be resentful, critical, and arrogant. I wanted to show him quickly how much more there was to life. I wanted immediate results. I felt like saying, 'Look at me, I know where it's at; you're asleep.' I wanted to shout and scream when he denied his feelings and continued to plug along in the rut we were in.

"For a while, I did all of these things. I ranted, raved, bragged, cajoled, pouted, sulked, and acted impulsively. In response, I got strain, anger, and tightness. More and more of what I didn't want. When things were at an all-time low, I called a very good friend of mine in Maine. I explained to her what had happened between Fred and me and what was happening to my marriage. Her response was simple. 'Let me see if I understand what you're saying, Julia,' she began. 'You've grown and expanded yourself through a loving and compassionate relationship. Now you are demanding that Bruce fit your image of an aware, adventurous, exciting, perceptive man. And you'd like him to meet your demand immediately and under duress. Is that it?' Well, I got the point.

"That was a year ago. After that conversation, I came down to earth. I began to respond positively when Bruce acted in a way I desired. I cut out the criticism. I prodded, but gently. I tried to provide the kind of nurturing Fred had provided for me. . . . Last night we had one of our best evenings ever, it was really marvelous and afterward, as we lay in bed having a cigarette and feeling very affectionate, Bruce began to talk about his feelings toward his father, about what his son meant to him, and about what he felt toward me. We talked, embraced, and cried in each other's arms until early morning. As far as I'm concerned, this was the first time we had made contact since we met nine years ago. You asked if my marriage was helped by an affair. The answer is no. Helped isn't strong enough. It was saved!"

RESEARCH, INFORMED OPINION, ETC.

Is Julia's description of the positive effect of her extra-relationship experience on her own growth and her marriage to be trusted? There is no reason to consider her experience less valid than those extra-relationship experiences that contribute to unproductive strain in a primary relationship. Of course, conclusions such as Julia's will draw many detractors. The late Dr. Abraham Stone would probably have been among them. Dr. Stone, a distinguished pioneer in family planning and marriage counseling, stated in an article published in *Readers Digest*, "From my quarter-century of counseling on marital problems, I cannot recall a single case where infidelity has strengthened the marital bond." Morton Hunt comments on Dr. Stone's statement in his book, *The Affair*, "Perhaps he, like many others with a similar view, came to this conclusion because he saw only troubled clients; perhaps infidelity was more deeply disturbing to many people a generation or so ago than it is today." A more recent study on the results of adultery in our society was conducted by gynecologist Dr. Lonny Meyers and the Reverend Hunter Leggitt. The conclusions they arrived at were published in the journal, *Sexual Behavior*. Based on their interviews they found that an affair enhances some relationships by:

- Lessening the feelings of resentment frequently found within the constraints of long-term relationships.
- Removing the burdens of sex and companionship from a spouse who may be exhausted, ill, preoccupied with other matters; or simply not in the mood.
- Increasing the warmth and excitement of one spouse, thereby stimulating the other.
- Motivating a person to become more attractive, to the spouse as well.
- Providing a diversion or temporary respite from marriage difficulties. This can bring a new perspective or tolerance to these problems.
- Assisting a person to discover new dimensions of his or her own sexuality and personality including (for women) orgasm, which may then for the first time be experienced also with the husband.

- Helping an unsatisfactory relationship to remain intact when there are other good reasons to continue the relationship, such as children, finances, and an established home base.

- Allowing persons to remain (or become) warm individuals despite cold relationships.

- By providing additional passion, tenderness, and stimulation for a person experiencing a good relationship.

Dr. Alfred Kinsey, in his volume on the American female, also looked at the other side of the story. He reported and cited three independent studies other than his own to support the statement that "sometimes there is an actual improvement of the marital relationship following extramarital experience." Morton Hunt formed a similar conclusion from his research: "Many psychotherapists and marriage counselors to whom I spoke said, in guarded terms, that stagnant marriages are sometimes stirred into life by the sharp new awareness the unfaithful person had gained of his or her needs, which leads him to make subtle new demands of his spouse and to respond positively when the other meets them." I have confirmed his finding in more recent conversations with my colleagues.

Of the people Hunt interviewed for his book (primarily white middle class, and geographically diverse), a small minority reported improved marital relationships as a result of their affairs: About one out of every ten interviewees said their first or some later affair had increased their sexual satisfactions within marriage; roughly the same number said it had brought them emotionally closer to their spouse; and one out of eight said it had strengthened the relationship by turning the partners back toward each other. The improvement seems more likely to be minor, or peripheral, in those cases where the deceived spouse never finds out, more likely to be major and central when the affair has been made known, and produced a searching reevaluation of the whole marital interaction.

REVERSALS AND RENEWALS

As we saw earlier, when an affair comes out in the open, it is almost always disruptive and usually destructive. But again, there are exceptions. Sometimes the relationship partners decide to repair and reconstruct their relationship and come up with a stronger, more mutually nurturant bond than they had before. It is quite possible they might never have done this without the stimulus of the affair.

Allen and Carole have been married thirteen years; four years ago a friend of Carole's told her that Allen was fooling around. At first, she didn't believe it, but when she confronted Allen, he admitted he had had an affair. In taking stock of the past four years, both Carole and Allen are mostly positive:

Carole: When I first found out about Allen's affair, I was shocked. I felt betrayed; it was as if I had been played for a fool. Things were pretty shaky between us for a long while, probably about a year or so. One of the things I had to admit, though, was that I wasn't really cheated. During the time of his affair, Allen wasn't distant and preoccupied, as unfaithful men are depicted in the movies. On the contrary, our sex life was heightened, and he was very affectionate.

Allen: I think that if a person with real integrity, a thoughtful person, feels that the growth of his personality and his happiness and welfare will be promoted by an affair, he should have it, because if he doesn't, he's going to cheat his mate! In the long run, he or she will sense an undercurrent of resentment, a feeling of duty rather than love that will be more destructive to life than a sexual experience with another, which leaves the lustier one, more content within the relationship. If I were I deprived of the affair during that period of my life, Carole would have become my enemy. . . . Nonetheless, being found out wasn't a picnic. I think one of the important factors that saved us is that our marriage really didn't have serious shortcomings. Friends of ours whose marriages are already rocky and unsatisfying had experienced extreme turmoil when an affair became an issue, and their marriages never recovered. My guess is that there wasn't much to salvage.

Carole: That first year was like recovering from an accident. Afterward, I came to see Allen and myself in a different light. First of all, I've learned the "wisdom of insecurity." Both men and women have a tendency after marriage to think, "The romance is over. I can sit back now; I've won him (or her) over." This leads to stagnation. There is a healthy drive toward self-improvement and maybe even a little competitiveness that ceases after marriage. This was revitalized by our marital difficulties.

Allen: In the last few years, I've come to appreciate Carole much more than previously. She has become more independent. I get a strong sense that she doesn't need me but she really wants me. She enjoys my company but isn't dependent on it or lost without me. If I were to disappear, she would be go on and continue handling her life well. I didn't sense that four years ago. That difference is really important to me. . . . Interestingly enough, nowadays Carole has orgasms nearly all the time, although before the affair she rarely did.

Carole: I would agree with Allen that I feel more independent as a person than I did four years ago, but I don't attribute it all to our marital difficulties, or at least not to the affair. What Allen is overlooking is that four years ago, I had two preschoolers to deal with. That will cut down on anyone's independence. Now that they are both off to school for a full day, I have started graduate school, and I can mingle in the civilized world. Like most mothers, I was going through a period of isolation and brain rot while Allen had his usual freedom. This is one of the things we've renegotiated. The responsibilities for the children and the house are shared now. . . . You know, though an extramarital affair isn't necessarily a disaster, it certainly isn't a panacea either.

Allen: I think you're right, Carole. The point is that a lot of things that have been very positive have occurred between us since that extramarital episode, and even though other factors may be equally important, the affair also played a critical role. Not that having an affair is going to bring anyone to glory, it's just that it doesn't necessarily kill, and in our case may have even provided a motivation for moving closer.

Carole: I agree. I wouldn't claim that we're completely happy now, but I would say that things are definitely better than before it all started.

After an affair is discovered, if the primary relationship does improve, it will probably do so only after considerable effort and agonizing. While the discovered affair is likely to be traumatic even if relationship differences are eventually resolved, relationship improvement when the affair is not discovered may come about with less or no trauma. In these cases, the outside experience, serving as a reality test of one's fantasy, may result in a new or renewed appreciation of one's mate.

In their book, *The Wandering Husband*, Dr. Hyman Spotnitz and writer Lucy Freeman take the general view that almost all infidelity is psychologically unhealthy. But even these conservatives recognize the exceptions and add, "We can make no ironclad rules, for there are instances where it may have saved a marriage. It may have convinced a husband that the other woman, far from being more desirable, is much less attractive than his wife."

If this insight can apply to wandering husbands, it can also apply to wandering wives. One such woman is Jennifer Lang. Mrs. Lang, at thirty-seven, has been married for eleven years. At first glance, she hardly seems like the sort who would turn to extra-relationship sex. A second-generation Irish Catholic, she is short and stocky, wears her sweaters a little too loosely, her curly black hair a little too short, and her shoes, chosen for comfort over style, do nothing to improve the appearance of her short muscular legs. Jennifer Lang's experience was expressed in a lengthy letter, which reads in part:

"There was a kind of growing dissatisfaction in my marriage that I couldn't put my finger on. Things were going along smoothly, the kids were doing fine, my husband was making decent money for the first time, and everybody was well. I couldn't understand my moodiness. Now, two years later, I have a better perspective. What happened was that my interests in life had broadened while my husband's had not, and at the same time, I was also moving away from my strong religious background while he remained devout and inhibited. Here I was, placing big value on affection and emotionality, while he seemed opposed to both. I was frustrated. As my discontent grew, I began to wonder what it would be like with another man. I fell into the habit of having long daydreaming sessions. I would even look forward to these private moments with my thoughts. What I did was create a fantasy involving a man with all the qualities I hungered for, openly and passionately emotional, adventurous, uninhibited. We would meet each other, embrace with real passion, and do all sorts of things together. I visualized dinner, dancing closely in each other's arms, kissing and lying tenderly in a soft, romantic embrace. I hardly ever fantasized lovemaking. Although I recognized it as part of the experience, the source of my dissatisfaction was not sexual, it was primarily emotional.

"Over the course of three years, I met and got to know three or four men. These are all men that I dated, two of them I slept with. They ranged from a bearded hippie playwright-cab driver to my gynecologist, who asked me out for a drink and with whom I related for a year, longer than any of the others. What I found out after getting to know these men is that my husband is a real find. Although some of these other guys are much more emotional and at times much more fun, this has its negative side. The playwright, for example, was the most affectionate, emotionally stimulating of them all. But on several occasions he didn't show up for dates or was so high that he wasn't coherent by the time he arrived, usually late! Sure, he had a spirited glint in his eye that was appealing, but it wasn't as exciting close up, then it was more bloodshot than sparkle! The gynecologist also had his drawbacks. At first, it was immensely flattering that my doctor found me attractive. I got a lot of ego inflation out of that. But after a while, I found him shallow and superficial. He's a great companion for dinner and light conversation. He's really an absorbing conversationalist as long as it's kept impersonal. Within a few months, though, his manner drove me wild. I found myself trying to reach this guy and he'd put on his frozen Calvinist face and become polite and monosyllabic. Then there was another one who sexually was dynamite. But that's all he was interested in. . . .

"All in all, I've concluded that my ideal of what a man 'should' be needs adjusting. My husband is sincere, responsible, in love with me, a good father, a sensitive lover, generous, and a little boring, too security-oriented, and over-conventional. Like everyone else, he has defects. So what! Christ, I've found that he has more going for him than most men. Those that were more exciting made horrible steady companions. I can really appreciate that now. The contrast has renewed my respect for my husband. I don't feel dissatisfied as I did before. Back several years ago, I felt my choice was to seek other men extra-maritally or to divorce. The option I chose worked for me."

PRONOUNCED DEAD

Jennifer Lang's marriage was lacking but viable. In relationships that are no longer salvageable, the third party may make the bankruptcy obvious. Before the appearance of the emotional, sexual competition, there were two very unhappy people. Afterward, with the marital bond formally split, each has a chance to embark on a new, more satisfying life. Here, one woman's experience:

"I'd been thinking about leaving my husband for four years but I was unsure of myself, afraid to face the single life, afraid of financial problems, afraid to face my parents, frightened that the whole thing was a mistake that I would regret forever. My fantasy was that no one else would ever want me if I left Robert. My marriage didn't seem worth a damn, but I really didn't have much basis for comparison. I was married very young, too young, actually, so I was naive. Also, Robert doesn't like to have people over and isn't very sociable at all, which cuts down my exposure to other couples. Being naive, underexposed, insecure, and unhappily married was one hell of a sorry state. . . . Our marriage never seemed any good. It included just about zero sex, and as far as I can see, it went on and on not only because of my fears but because of Robert's fears also. He was an up-and-coming corporate lawyer who felt pretense was important; rather than admitting to his colleagues, our parents, and our friends that we couldn't stand each other, he plodded along smiling in public and ignoring me in private, 'It's what's up front that counts.'"

"One weekend with Phil changed everything. Not that I had any hopes of marrying him, he was too happily married for that. We met at the library several times and one weekend he asked jokingly if I wanted to keep him company on a business trip. He may have been joking, but I wasn't. I jumped at the opportunity. In that one weekend, I learned so much about my own feelings, and my ability to relate to a man on every level. The exhilaration, expansiveness, and sense of discovery that I experienced with Phil gave a new direction to my life. I thought of myself in a completely new way. I almost hugged myself, and cried for all the years I had wasted thinking that I didn't have the capacity to be happy. . . . Sexually, I had never responded as I did with Phil. In my marriage, the lovemaking was wordless, perfunctory, and swift. Phil was a warm and enthusiastic lover. From the moment we touched and kissed, we were pulled to each other; we were key and lock, melody and harmony, cerebral and physical, playful and serious. We made love all weekend. I was never as sharply aware of my sexuality. I was like a wild beast in heat; my body was constantly eager and vibrant. He was only too willing to comply. He rejoiced at the opportunity; it was extraordinarily exciting.

"We made love every night for the following week. On the last night of the week, I broke into tears after I came. I was ready. I went and told my husband everything in a great emotional scene and moved out that same night. I'm living alone now. My marriage is behind me. Sometimes I'm very lonely but I'm happier. The singles scene can be dehumanizing. The bars, clubs, online dating, Facebook, etc., everything is so plastic. But I have no regrets. I have an exciting job. I've met men I could love, and I feel capable of making myself happy, that was my precious find."

Just as some relationships are exposed in all their sterility by an affair, others, just as empty, may be given artificial life by outside involvements. Rather than face the bleakness of their marriage and courageously arrange for a separation or a divorce, some couples stick their heads in the sand and carry on desultory affairs. After a few years of this, there are often bitter regrets—"I should have ended it when I was younger" or "I've thrown away the best years of my life." Once more, we can see the dual edge of extramarital involvement, it can work both ways, for us or against us.

PLAYING THE ODDS: ISSUE AND ANSWERS

We have seen that an affair may be destructive in intent, designed to get rid of a mate; a chance by-product of other relationship problems; have little to do with the mate at all; be employed to arouse the partner's interest; be based on revenge for real or fancied hurts; be a way-station on a route back to a more solid marriage. The affair can be a cry for help, a reaching out for health, or the acting out of an inner disturbance. It may be used to prop up a relationship that might better be dissolved, or be the final straw that breaks the bond of a corrupt coupling.

People who have liberal attitudes about adultery in general may surprise themselves when the abstraction becomes a reality in their own relationship. Others, though conservative in theory, may be forgiving and compassionate. Those who respond initially with mild upset may have a more serious delayed reaction. Some partners are truly devastated and rocked to the very foundations of their personality. We know now that there are many kinds of relationships and many kinds of adultery, that all monogamy is not blissful and healthy and that all adultery is not painful and sick. The partner who is having an affair may become more open, more in touch with his or her feelings. At the time of the affair, the involved partner may make a greater effort to please the other partner, thereby affecting a temporary (and occasionally a lasting) improvement in the relationship. Variety may be introduced into the primary relationship's sex life by the unfaithful partner who has gained a new sexual outlook or learned some new flirty ways of being. Some unfaithful partners develop a stronger appreciation and love for their spouses as a result of extra-relationship activity.

These are the potential positive effects of an affair. Suspicion, anger, distrust, guilt, and even divorce are more common negative effects. In traditional relationships without close communication between the mates, more negative disruption tends to occur if the wife's affair is discovered, especially if it is sexual, rather than exclusively emotional. If the husband has an affair, less harm seems to result, especially if it is sexual, rather than "just" emotional, but "less" is nowhere near neutral.

What sense can we make of these seeming contradictions? An affair tends to make life more exciting; whether or not it satisfies, produces conflict, destroys, or uncovers a new dimension of personality it certainly intensifies life. Beyond that, we can only say one thing with certainty: all general conclusions are likely to have notable exceptions!

Some relationships gain from adultery, others lose; some mates grow, others deteriorate; occasionally the effects of an affair are temporary and of no real consequence, other times they have critical impact and are long-lasting. There are very few reliable scientific studies on the positive aspects of an affair. With a few exceptions, those that have been done have sampled populations that are either biased in a liberal or conservative direction, depending on the consequences the questioner wanted to emphasize. This is not legitimate research. More objective evidence and clinical investigation of non-patient populations by and large echo the conclusions noted in earlier chapters: That adultery must adversely affect a marriage or that it is *always* a symptom of a troubled relationship or troubled psyche is an overstatement. A number of factors play out in a discovered affair, including the state of the relationship, the motivation of the adulterer, the self-regard and internal strength of the noninvolved spouse (particularly if the affair is discovered), and the meaning the affair holds for both spouses.

Considering all these factors, the majority of professionals who have published opinions and I myself conclude that prolonged extra-relationship experiences result in decidedly more negative than positive effects on a primary relationship. Consider it this way: In a mutually tender, loving relationship, the stakes rise; there is more to lose and less to gain. Yet, paradoxically, the likelihood of losing a truly solid relationship is smaller. In a non-satisfactory relationship that one desires to keep intact, there is less to lose and more to gain, but if found out, the likelihood is that the relationship facade will quickly drop. These are the extremes; most relationships lie in between.

Sound Thinking and Smart Moves

1. It would be a mistake if the takeaway to this chapter is seen as a rationale to have an affair. While positive effects are a possible outcome as we've seen, the behavior involves lying, subterfuge, a huge breach of trust, and it is usually the basis of a significant degree of grief by the uninvolved partner, even if there is an eventual happy ending.

2. Considering the longer life span enjoyed in Western countries such as the United States, the challenge is for couples to grow as individuals throughout the life span. It is about staying interested, and interesting. We would be wise to view our relationship similarly to a car on a hill—it must be in forward gear, or else it will quite naturally head south.

3. If an affair is going to create "a new start," it is going to depend on strong relationship skills going forward, which involves overlearning. Practicing a new and positive relationship habit, like making positive comments, or responding empathetically far beyond the point where you can do it well, greatly reduces the likelihood that you will revert to the old habits of relating that do not foster relationship prosperity.

Chapter 6

HEALING AND IMPROVING A RELATIONSHIP AFTER AN AFFAIR

WHAT ONCE WAS

The scene is an exclusive seaside restaurant. A forty-something couple are having dinner. He is deeply tanned, prosperous looking. She, a former model, now a PhD candidate in English literature, has bright green eyes, and a lightly freckled face under a fluff of reddish-brown hair. They have been married eighteen years. They are aware of each other but only vaguely.

This night, as on many others in the past year, their attention is directed elsewhere; presently their eyes and ears are trained on a young couple seated nearby, a man and a women locked in each other's gaze, speaking softly, inaudibly, sometimes laughing together, other times looking very serious, playful, and earnest, all the while holding hands.

The older couple disconnected for many years, share a silent thought: Can we ever get past the affair—his, and hers in revenge? Looking back both thought they had talked out their relationship issues and were past those difficult events. What did they miss? In-depth interviews with individuals who had experienced infidelity have revealed a three-stage process following disclosure of an affair (Olson et al., 2002).

The process of healing starts with an "emotional roller coaster" and moves through a "moratorium" before efforts at trust building, the third stage, are initiated. This couple is stuck in the moratorium stage. They have touched on other critical issues, like mutual empathy, forgiveness, and rebuilding of trust, but their efforts were insufficient. Their breach of trust is like an infection that was not completely cleaned out. It still festers but their emotional distance has become normalized.

They continue together in desperation, ignoring their failure to share their feelings. There is a marked absence of empathy, the single most important ingredient of intimacy—and critical to healing, for both partners. Repeatedly failing to connect with each other, their feelings have turned into going along to get along, but the fire they once had has banked.

Most committed relationships rest on a foundation of trust, whether stated explicitly or assumed and implicit. Supporting the importance of trust, Bachand and Caron (2001) surveyed "good" marriages and found that partners in these relationships rated as most important "trust in each other that includes fidelity, integrity and feeling safe" as well as a "permanent commitment to the marriage."

Reversing the trend of mistrust in a primary relationship and taking steps toward healing a major breach is essential if the couple's connection is to be restored. When an affair either comes out in the open or, undiscovered, is symptomatic of a poorly functioning relationship, the relationship partners may decide to repair and reconstruct their relationship. Some couples try it on their own, others with professional help. Self-help is risky; even with the support of a well-trained mental health practitioner, considerable time, skill, and effort are required to achieve healing. Patience, courage, and the persistent desire to change are important ingredients, but much more is required.

HEALING: SELF-SOOTHING, AS A USEFUL TOOL

As we've seen in previous examples, when an affair has been discovered, the immediate reaction is likely to be distress and harsh feelings directed toward the offender. During the initial therapy sessions, crisis management is going to be necessary. Couples are likely to be overwhelmed with feelings of depression, anxiety, shame, and rage that make direct interactions difficult. As a result, interaction is best directed to the therapist, rather to each other.

It is the therapist's challenge to support each partner without alienating either; no small task. In an effort to get past this emotional roller coaster, it is often helpful to provide tools for self-soothing: Self-soothing does not involve overindulgence, emotional regression, or food or substance bingeing. It does involve taking care of yourself while you're stretching your personal boundaries or simply going through a difficult time.

Self-soothing permits you to quiet and calm yourself; it is self-care but not self-indulgence. The process requires that you not give up on yourself, or tell yourself it is too hard to settle your emotions down. It may be hard but not too hard. You have to stick with yourself, just as you would with a friend going through a difficult time.

Here are some suggestions for self-soothing that have been successfully used in clinical practice:

- If you are having a hard time, reduce the number and complexity of tasks confronting you by notifying those around you, including your children, to temporarily make fewer demands. Work-related projects and extra responsibilities (e.g., volunteer activities), which add to a hectic, pressured schedule, should be postponed for the time being. In a sense, an ailing psyche, like an ailing body, requires special attention and energy until it is strengthened.

- If your stress is coming from a relationship, you may have to reduce contact to self-repair when the exchange is consistently too unsettling. At the very least, attempt to do less together and enjoy it more rather than the reverse. The duration and degree of physical separation are determined by your emotional state: How badly are you feeling and how quickly can you recover from contact? Make it clear that your time-out is for self-repair, not withdrawal. Once replenished, you are in a better position to renew your efforts to regain your relationship connection.

- Do your best to stop the negative mental tapes. Stop "awfulizing" the situation and/or telling yourself, "How could this happen to me!" Accept the present reality and settle down. Quiet yourself instead of exacerbating your very emotional state and losing perspective.

- To help regulate your emotions, look at your past history and recall challenges that you faced successfully. Remind yourself that you are resilient. If you can't regulate your emotions, control your behavior. Once again, try to regain some perspective; reactions and situations don't last forever. Behave in a productive manner that you'll respect afterward, even if your emotions suggest otherwise. In other words, ask yourself, "If I felt better, how would I handle this?" Then, do your best to at least approximate that behavior. In contrast, when you start saying, "Maybe I shouldn't do that, but . . ." or "Maybe I shouldn't say that but . . ." take your own advice.

- One of the most effective things you can do to self-sooth is to write about the situation that has you stressed. Set aside some time, and write a letter to yourself or to others who are involved in your distress. No one needs to see these letters but you; so don't hold back, censor yourself, or worry about how well the letter is written. Just put all the hurt and rage that's been festering inside and contaminating your system on the page. You may also want to write a letter to yourself. An important aspect of self-soothing is to stop punishing yourself for past mistakes. Instead, write a letter of forgiveness. Look back at regrettable actions; recall who you were at the time. Remind yourself that you are a work in progress, ever evolving, always learning, and fallible. Perfection isn't for human beings.

- Create a peaceful place inside you. If you can tap that source, you can stop distress from building up, allowing your mind to clear and focus more sharply. There are numerous ways to create calm: yoga, meditation, a walk in nature, a hot aromatic bath, a good massage, soothing music, prayer, deep breathing, pleasant memories, and so on.

Do not expect the aforementioned suggestions to be easily or quickly soothing. When the wound is deep, as it is in a breach of trust, the greatest trap is to expect too much healing to happen too soon. Particularly during a period when the hurt is acute, it is wise for those more extroverted to fortify yourself on the nourishment that friends and individual interests provide. For those more inclined to introversion, sometimes some solitary time is best. In either case, it is a judgment call based on self-knowledge.

FORGIVING, STARTING THE PROCESS

In time, when couples are able to speak directly to each other in a constructive manner, the interaction is shifted to each other, rather than through the therapist. Strong emotions are understandable, given the gravity of the issue, but if the relationship and the individuals are to heal, at some point an attitude shift is necessary, the process of forgiveness needs to be considered, each partner needs to question him or herself:

> Are you for your partner or against your partner? This may sound like a strange question in light of the circumstance, and it is certainly not the initial question, but for healing to occur, at some point with emotional readiness, it must be answered. If healing is to occur it must be answered positively. After an affair, even long after, many people in relationships act like they are enemies. They put a negative spin on each other, just as enemies do.

If you decide you want to love your partner, you can choose to view him or her lovingly. You can choose to do things that make you feel good about each other, instead of acting in a manner that pokes holes in the relationship. Your partner's actions are subject to your explanation; we all give meaning to the behavior we view. Why not attribute a positive explanation to your partner's behavior whenever possible? Often a positive explanation is just as valid as one that leaves you feeling less connected. Research suggests that how you think about your partner, that is, how you explain your partner's behavior to yourself will be a critical factor for the well-being of your relationship, and that also applies to both the affair-involved and noninvolved partner.

Is this to suggest that a partner's affair should be viewed positively or somehow less than an assault on trust? It must be noted that explaining your partner to yourself with a more positive, rather than more negative slant does not mean to forget, excuse, or condone the offense. In other words, viewing one's partner with compassion does not absolve him or her of responsibility for their actions but it can help to relieve both partners of burdensome emotions that preclude individual and relationship healing. Being clear on the meaning of viewing your partner positively, the way you do for your children or a dear friend can do much to begin the healing process.

While forgiveness is understandably a hard proposition for the noninvolved partner to consider early on, at some point of readiness it needs to be considered. Evidence-based treatments for healing relationships post-affair involve several factors, including forgiveness. Fife et al. (2008a) contend that forgiveness is a critical factor in primary relationships. Other clinical researchers note that individuals and families with the ability to ask for and grant forgiveness for significant interpersonal mistreatment are more likely to experience satisfying family relationships and emotional and physical health (Battle & Miller, 2005). Fincham et al. (2006) indicate that forgiveness is positively associated with several aspects of relationships such as intimacy, affect, and relationship satisfaction. They also suggest that levels of forgiveness are likely to predict relationship conflict and psychological aggression toward the partner following an offense.

As discussed here, forgiveness is an interaction between the forgiving person, the offending person, and the relationship between them; it is interactional, involving both partners. As previously cited by Fincham et al. (2006), when applied and accepted by patients, forgiveness facilitates affective, cognitive, and behavioral changes for both the unfaithful and the betrayed partner. In other words, the model involves both partners in the challenge of healing.

Ultimately, forgiveness helps couples heal relationship wounds, renew attachment security, and rebuild a sense of unity, resulting in significant changes at the core of the relationship (Butler et al., 2009). In short, the interpersonal model of forgiveness helps restore couples to a state of togetherness by requiring them to work as a couple through the forgiveness process. In contrast, without forgiveness both partners are going to suffer and the relationship is likely to fail.

FACILITATING FORGIVENESS: EMPATHY

Empathy is a primary and assisting factor leading to forgiveness. Empathy is a shift in attention from one's own experience toward the experience of one's partner and involves an active effort to understand another person's perception of an interpersonal event as if one were in that other person's shoes—this is critical to forgiveness. Further, empathy opens the door for couples to begin reconnecting and bridging the chasm that results from infidelity.

Empathy, while powerful, is quite likely to be difficult to accomplish for couples who have experienced an affair. Both partners are often consumed with their own emotions after the affair has been revealed. However, if the therapist regularly models empathy and coaches couples, the chance of it catching on is increased. Hearing the pain and anger of the betrayed partner can be difficult and there is a tendency for couples to become defensive during empathy attempts. However, it is important to reduce defensiveness early on so that unfaithful partners can be open, acknowledge their wrongdoing, accept responsibility for the betrayal, and experience empathy for their partner. Feeling empathy for the pain that one has caused will eventually help the guilty party express remorse and offer a genuine apology.

When exploring the relational context of the affair therapists should help betrayed partners to develop empathy as well. Both partners are likely to have experienced pain and sorrow in the relationship and a mutual understanding of the other's experience can promote increased unity and healing. When the timing is right, a therapist may invite the partner who had broken the trust to reflect on the pain and sorrow their partner has experienced in the relationship betrayal. They too may have experienced disappointments and unmet longings for connection and intimacy in the relationship that will require discussion in time.

Recognizing the pain and suffering of another can have a softening effect. The experience and expression of empathy provides an important balm for healing the wounds that partners have respectively experienced. Another way to promote empathy is to ask couples to recount the situation from each other's point of view (Worthington, 1998). Experiencing sincerely felt empathy from one increases the likelihood of it being reciprocated by the other partner. That is, as unfaithful partners communicate their understanding of the pain they caused with the affair, betrayed partners may begin to soften in their expression of anger or intense questioning. In turn, offending partners may experience a decrease in defensiveness as they feel their partners are being more empathic and less focused on expressing blame and resentment.

The least popular but most constructive method of coping with the heightened emotions regarding the discovery of an affair is to face it squarely and openly discuss the feelings and implications involved. In the following dialogue, Dori and Alvin, whom we met in an earlier chapter, are beginning to communicate about his extramarital affair. They are in their early forties. Recall, several weeks previously Dori discovered that Alvin was having an affair. This exchange is after several treatment sessions. For the most part, the initial emotional crisis has been significantly diminished allowing a focus on speaking about the issues empathetically.

Alvin: Dori, I am really bothered about the strain and emotional gap between us.

Dori: Did I start it?

Alvin: (Deflecting, rather than being defensive) Drop that for a minute. The point is we're both unhappy, and if we just continue to drag on with blaming and counter-blaming, it will end up in a divorce. If that happens, there's no guarantee that either of us will be better off. A lot of men are worse than I am, and I still prefer you to any woman I know.

Dori: Thanks. I'll tell Florence Jackson that the next time I see her.

Alvin: (again, avoiding the temptation of being sucked into a destructive argument) I hurt you. I'm sorry. Very sorry. We have two children to consider. Their lives are also at stake here.

Dori: Does that scare you?

Alvin: Yes, it does. I am concerned that we work this out for them as well as for ourselves. I want to tell you how I feel about what has happened. We really haven't talked about it yet, just around it.

Dori: A little psychology lecture coming up?

Alvin: (Maintaining a conciliatory attitude) Maybe. Anyway, Dori, I feel very badly about what happened. I know you've been hurt and you're angry. I understand that. I want you to know that Florence really didn't mean that much to me; you've got it over her by a mile.

Dori: Oh, so you've come back to me on a rebound. Things didn't work out too well with Florence, is that it?

Alvin: No. Things could have worked out, but I didn't want to split. I want to be with you.

Dori: Well, I guess that's a compliment; in a backhand sort of way.

Alvin: On top of feeling guilty about all that's happened, up to now I've been getting defensive every time the issue comes up; I even feel tense in anticipation of it coming up. I get mad and accuse you of a lot of things that are really petty; spreading the blame around and taking it off me. Not good!

Dori: Are you apologizing? (Dori is beginning to change her reaction from sarcasm to sympathy in response to Alvin's persistent, honest, nondefensive stance.)

Alvin: Yes. You know, I think, that this is difficult for me.

Dori: Yes, I do. Thanks.

Alvin: Your bitterness and bitchy attitude since you found out haven't made things any easier. It's hard to discuss my feelings if every time I open my mouth, I get walloped. (Alvin is beginning to define the issues blocking their communication.)

Dori: (nondefensively) How would you feel in my place? I felt humiliated and scared. Florence is five years younger than me; I felt as if I were being discarded for a newer model. I have felt old and ugly. Up to then I felt secure in our relationship. (For the first time, Dori is revealing very personal, painful feelings directly, without attacking.)

Alvin: (softly, compassionately) Why did you try to hide those feelings from me?

Dori: I felt so vulnerable; I was protecting myself. I didn't feel safe with you. I still don't trust you as before. I know you've been trying to reach me; I agree that my attitude has made it harder.

Alvin: I understand more now of what's been going on inside of you, Dori.

In this dialogue, as contrasted with their earlier one in the previous chapter, Alvin and Dori are less defensive, with Alvin leading the way by example. They are beginning to explore openly and honestly feelings about each other and about Alvin's affair. This is very difficult for Dori, who initially was sarcastic, angry, and defensive. Several times Alvin could have been pulled into a nasty, counterproductive argument. Rather than expressing her feelings and wants directly, Dori began by being hostile through her sarcasm, but to his credit Alvin didn't get drawn into doing the same.

When anger reins, each conversation ends in a disruption; there is a lack of honest expression of feelings. Trust is not restored by these bouts and the fighting is likely to continue until the relationship is torn apart or has seriously deteriorated. Since these encounters are so sensitive, the communication is likely to be nonproductive unless one partner is able to stick to the problem at hand—that is, the hurt feelings, misunderstandings, and anger, as Alvin did (". . . the point is we're both unhappy"), even in the midst of blame-oriented messages ("Did I start it?"), such as Dori began with. Understanding Dori's feelings as well as being honest about his own, and forgoing the temptation to counterattack, Alvin was able to create an atmosphere where Dori felt safe enough to express herself honestly. There may be a long way to go, but that is a beginning.

RESTORING TRUST

In relationships, as in business, trust is like a bridge that enables us to connect with each other. In love relationships, we feel safe enough to attain intimacy when the bridge is solid and we are confident of its support. When trust is undermined and we feel disappointed or betrayed, such as when we are deceived by a lie, exploited by a broken promise, or disappointed by the discrepancy between what is said and done, we pull back just as we would do on a bridge that has become unsteady. Our expectations are shattered. We may be so shaken that trust in our own judgment is undermined. We feel a sense of loss that a loved one didn't respect us enough to be honest or fulfill a promise (Block, 2001).

A broken trust filters down to children. Using a sample of adult children whose parents committed infidelity, Nogales (2009) found that 80 percent of participants' attitudes toward love and relationship were influenced by their parent's infidelity. The same study also found that 70 percent of participants reported that their parent's infidelity had inhibited or reduced their ability to trust their romantic partners. Trust plays a vital role in the establishment and maintenance of healthy and satisfying relationships.

Gottman (2011) states, "Happier couples, for whom trust was not missing, described the concept of trust as the mysterious quality that somehow created safety, security, and openness for both of them" (p. 39). Trust also impacts one's willingness to safely explore his or her sexuality (Gottman, 2011). Among adult children exposed to parental infidelity, a weakened or nonexistent sense of trust may inhibit their ability to experience a heightened sense of sexual curiosity and limit their willingness to accept guidance and support from romantic partners. Individuals who experience less trust in their relationship are more likely to engage in infidelity (Cramer et al., 2000). Consistent with this, adult children exposed to infidelity in their childhood are more likely to engage in infidelity within their own romantic relationships (Fish et al., 2012; Nogales, 2009; Platt et al., 2008).

In short, a broken trust is a weakened bridge that we can no longer cross, leaving us scrambling to search for the safety of solid ground. In some cases, we may feel terrified that we are losing control over our lives, since we don't know where to turn for support.

Trust means different things to different people—dependability, loyalty, honesty, fidelity, predictability. But at its heart is feeling physically secure and emotionally safe. When we trust someone, we are able to express our deepest feelings and fears; we can reveal who we are and what we need, knowing the other person will accept us, regard our feelings, and protect us. In turn, our trustworthy partner is likely to feel confident to do the same, knowing we will respond in kind. In essence, when we trust someone and act on that trust, we are giving that person a piece of ourselves, believing they will be understanding, caring, and honor our faith in them.

Some mistakenly think when trust stemming from an affair is resolved it is over. However, once trust has been broken, integrity must be woven into the entire fabric of the relationship. Especially after an affair is discovered, the non-involved partner needs to be able to trust in an all-inclusive way counting on their partner to be reliable, honest, keep promises, and act in their best interest. While a small, isolated breach of trust may have minor impact ordinarily, this is not the case after trust has been violated in a major way. Infidelity trumps the smaller breaches of trust, but it magnifies the effect of smaller breaches as well.

When trust is breached as a result of an affair, the disappointed partner is often so shaken that it creates an overall feeling of insecurity in the relationship. That is the power of trust betrayed. It spreads throughout the entire relationship like a deadly toxin.

Partners who are serious in repairing their relationship are behaving in a manner that has a higher probability that their sustained credibility will grow into integrity. They are frank, acknowledging their feelings, even feelings that express shortcomings, "I have been preoccupied with my work lately and I know I haven't been as attentive"—which contributes to their aura of authenticity. Being reliable and consistent, including acknowledging shortcomings, promotes credibility and will help to restore their partner's view of their integrity. In contrast, partners who are not forthright and who are unreliable undermine credibility and are likely to be disappointed with their partner's view of their credibility and integrity.

For instance, Kevin and Janice, two technology consultants who are both remarried are on the verge of splitting because Janice contends that Kevin "never lives up to his word." Here's what Janice said about some troubling events nearly two years after she found out about an affair:

"I can't believe anything he tells me anymore. I ask him if he's taken care of the dentist bill and he assures me that he has. The next thing I know, the dental office is calling and asking me about the overdue balance. That type of thing has happened several times already. Or I ask him to do me a favor. He agrees and then doesn't come through."

As Janice described it, when she complained to Kevin about his behavior, their conversation went like this:

Kevin:	There you go, exaggerating again. I was only late with a bill once. Maybe twice. And I knew you'd bug me if I told you the truth. The same thing with the favors. Sometimes I say yes just so you'll get off my case. Do I have a life sentence because of the fling?
Janice:	So now you're telling me that you purposely lie to me and it's my fault because I bug you. And, I should no longer be shaken after all the lies in the past about *her*?
Kevin:	I'm just saying that sometimes you drive me crazy, and at those times, especially if I'm feeling tired or something, I'll do anything to get relief.
Janice (sarcastically):	Driving you crazy? That's great. Now I can never trust what you tell me, because it may be one of those times that you simply think the truth isn't necessary. What else aren't you telling me?

At this point, Janice explained that she felt so disappointed and insecure by Kevin's lack of candor that she no longer trusted him in any area of their life and was ready to leave. Kevin pleaded with her to reconsider and she did, on the condition that she and Kevin resolve their differences.

Kevin agreed to discuss their relationship and talk honestly about what bothered him as well as listen to Janice's concerns. In their discussion it became clear that Kevin had chosen the convenience of "yessing" Janice at the expense of his credibility. By talking openly for the first time, and implementing a plan to strengthen trust, they established a renewed bond.

Janice and Kevin's relationship illustrates that being inconsistent or unreliable is almost certain to undermine a relationship, especially when an infidelity is part of their history. Inconsistency is present when a partner speaks and acts in contradictory ways. If one partner tells the other, "You are the most important person in my life and my top priority," but in daily behavior is selfish, inconsiderate, and irritable, how can the words be trusted? Actions speak more forcefully and belie the words. Sincerity counts!

Building toward greater honesty and increased trust involves not simply saying what one believes but doing what one says. A person who wants to be counted on must be reliable and consistent in both words and behaviors. One must "walk the talk," as they say.

Frequently, partners who have difficulties in following through on their word are motivated by temporary feelings of guilt ("She seems so upset,

I better do this. . ."), or require the approval of their partner ("I better say yes; he seems terribly angry about this"). The problem is the lack of follow through if their partner isn't emotional, which creates a negative emotional cycle. Others acquiesce so that their partner will "get off my back." As we've seen with Janice and Kevin, the relief is short-lived, only to be replaced by their partner's rage. It is not about pacifying, it is about integrity.

The same effect of insecurity is often produced by vague statements: "I agree that I need to be more attentive" or "Okay, I'll be more responsive." In the former, the speaker does not indicate a willingness to do something different; the latter statement avoids a specific plan of action and is likely to be just another empty statement that weakens trust.

On other occasions, suspicion arises not so much by what is said, but by how it is said. Larry may say to his wife, "I'm listening," while glancing at the morning newspaper. Rita, Larry's wife, has good cause to wonder about the reliability of Larry's statement.

Larry was obviously more interested in the morning's news than in conversing with Rita. Larry could have said, "Couldn't we wait till later?" If Rita felt strongly about talking, she could have made this known. If she didn't, she could have respected Larry's desire to delay the conversation.

Larry and Rita were being overly polite in an attempt to create an impression that is unreasonable: We are both *always* desirous of contact with each other. In actuality, both Larry and Rita were collecting resentment and undermining the trust in the relationship.

TAKING TRUST REPAIR SERIOUSLY

If trust is to be restored and kept intact, secrets are to be avoided. Secrets come in all sizes, degrees of complexity, and forms. And secrets are not uncommon. More than 60 percent of married people have kept secrets from their spouses according to recent research (Easterling et al., 2012).

There are two main ways for the offender (and the offended) to make things worse when confronted with a trust violation: One is withdrawal, to keep everything bottled up inside. The other is to erupt, to emote without restraint. If you are having too many conversations with yourself, you are probably not having enough with your partner. If you are screaming, hurling insults, and looking to vent without concern for the impact, not briefly, but mostly, the relationship is certain to deteriorate.

Bear in mind: a critical action on the trust-breaker's part, as reassurance that his efforts to restore trust are sincere, is his willingness to delve into himself, confront the personal issues that lead to trust breaches, and acknowledge them openly and responsibly.

To begin, an unequivocal apology is in order. No excuses, no "buts," no mitigating circumstances. The apology is something like, "I am very sorry that I behaved in an irresponsible manner, that I betrayed your faith in me by deceiving you." It is not something like, "I'm sorry you're upset about my behavior but if you were more affectionate I wouldn't have done what I did."

The former is the statement of an adult who realizes that he is in charge of his life, and the consequences of his actions. The latter is the statement of a child who still believes that he is a victim of other people or circumstances. Unless he changes his view and begins to take charge of his life, the chances that he will be a trustworthy partner are near zero. Other considerations:

1. Following an apology, is the discussion, or more likely a series of discussions with the goal of understanding the basis for trust violations. Simply stated, "Why has this happened, and what is going to happen that will prevent a recurrence?" Understanding the basis for a breach of trust does not guarantee that it won't happen again. However, unless there is a belief in magic, it is unreasonable to assume that trust violations will not recur without addressing the reasons they have occurred and formulating a prevention plan.

2. Some questions to pose for a discussion: What influences from our family of origin may be undermining our relationship? What changes need to be made in the relationship to strengthen the trust and intimacy? Very specifically, what kinds of behaviors are acceptable and what are out of bounds? Can the damage be repaired? What, specifically, will it take? What are the hopes and expectations for the future?

3. While talking is critical, it is not enough. Behavioral patterns require change as well. In the past, for example, the partner who has violated the trust may have come home at night, barely mumbled a hello as he was reviewing the mail, made some small talk during dinner and retired to the TV to watch the ball game for the remainder of the evening. That routine is not much of a relationship promoter under any circumstance and definitely won't cut it in the wake of a breach of trust.

4. The offending partner needs to think through exactly what he'd like to see happen in the relationship and behave in a manner that promotes his vision. Regardless of the specifics, the general message his behavior should convey is, "I love you. You matter to me. I want to demonstrate that I am trustworthy." This may require a shift in the usual manner of behaving and in the daily routine; it can be a lot of work, a real stretch for some people. If a serious trust issue is to be repaired it can only happen in the context of a caring environment. It is up to the offending partner to create that atmosphere, even if it is at some sacrifice.

5. The reparative behaviors required might be new and a stretch, but they do not have to be sensational. Indeed, some people are so preoccupied with major shifts that opportunities for small but important gestures are overlooked. Others mistakenly believe that a repair process moves along on its own energy and consequently do not bother to fuel it at all. These individuals are the same as those who seem to sidestep escalating conflict by sweeping the incident under the rug and acting as if it hadn't occurred. It may appear as if conflict has been safely avoided in these instances. Appearances notwithstanding, there is no avoidance of trust violations without negative consequences.

6. Just as relationship-supporting behaviors need to be strengthened, there are also trust-specific requirements to be considered. Common requests are for greater accountability, consistency, reliability, and sacrifice. Especially in instances where there has been an affair, accountability may involve an accurate itinerary during travel, calls during the day and coming home from work in time to have dinner with the family. It goes without saying that the trust-violating behavior in question must stop completely. No more contact with a lover, for example.

7. In addition to accountability most trust-damaged lovers require consistency and reliability to be present in a much greater degree than had been the case. Being clear about intentions and keeping agreements, even those that seem minor, such as calling when promised are very important. Once the trust wound has been exposed, sensitivity is increased and must be respected.

8. Some couples also request that monthly bank statements, credit card statements, and phone bills are made available. Other couples insist on therapy, and a complete and detailed description of the trust violations. Yet, others need some time for intimate talk and reassurance each day. The specific requests vary from person to person but in all cases they should be in the service of helping the hurt partner feel more cared for, appreciated, and emotionally secure. And that's how the trust-breaking partner should view them, rather than as punitive and arbitrary.

9. Strengthening trust is not a one-person endeavor. The offended partner shares in the responsibility of the repair process. In fact, if there isn't receptiveness to the possibility of trusting again, and an encouragement of the offender's efforts to restore confidence, the process is destined to failure. An "indefinite sentence" or a prolonged period of coldness and alienation, perhaps going on for months, will almost surely result in the offended partner giving up in his efforts to reconnect. It is most helpful, in contrast, to consider carefully what is needed to restore trust, spell it out (not globally, like "be more reliable," but specifically, like, "call when you say you will") and collaborate with the offender in creating a blueprint for reparation.

Olson et al. (2002) in their research on infidelity asked their research participants, all of whom had experienced infidelity in their relationships, what advice they would offer to other men and women going through this difficult experience, here is what they suggested:

- Really listen to one another, to try and really understand where they are coming from.
- Don't hold anything back, but at the same time don't yell and scream.
- Find someone to talk to outside of the marriage.
- Stay around positive people.
- Don't make any quick decisions.
- If you choose to forgive someone, forgive them. You can't constantly bring it up.

Realistically, being responsive to an offending partner's efforts when there has been a betrayal, or pattern of deception is a major challenge. In these instances, the negative feelings come easily and will not yield easily: simply thinking about the relationship differently, although important, is not powerful enough. More is needed. Behavior must change toward each other and *both* partners must be committed to the repair process. It takes two to put the repair of trust on a healing path.

Sound Thinking and Smart Moves

1. In order for treatment to have a chance at being successful, it is necessary for the affair-involved partner to cut off all contact with the third party. In that regard, the affair-involved partner needs to accede to the noninvolved partner's requests to provide passwords in order to view phone records and other histories as aid to restore trust. Openness facilitates healing, secrecy opposes it. Consequently, the affair-involved partner needs to concede privacy, at least until trust is stabilized, and that concession needs to be given graciously.

2. While the noninvolved partner is likely to have a host of questions, it is unwise to answer those that are graphic, for example, "Did you do—sexually?" Answers to these questions leave images that frequently linger and add to damaged feelings as well as increase trauma.

3. Discussion about the affair by the relationship partners should not evolve into a "life sentence" for the involved, and the noninvolved partner. A healthy relationship is thwarted by unending discussion of one partner's fallibility. With the assistance of the treating therapist, a liberal time limit for discussion and treatment of the issue should be set and adhered to.

Chapter 7

CHILDREN: MINIMIZING THE DISRUPTION

PARENTING

Being a parent, as Sigmund Freud once remarked, is an impossible profession under even the best of circumstances. Parental discord can escalate the difficulties to unbearable limits. When three generations of family members lived in the same house or nearby, it was easier to raise children. Grandmothers and aunts could counsel and help a mother who was distressed; a couple who needed time to themselves to work out their differences could ask another adult they trusted to take over for a while. Husband and wife could discuss their issues with older and frequently wiser members of their family. And the children could find a loving adult with time to listen and to counsel, a sort of court of appeals. Today's parents often share the responsibility for being everything to their children.

Childless couples can sometimes reconcile their relationship differences and disappointments by ignoring the discords, pretending they do not exist. They can seek compensating gratifications elsewhere, perhaps in their work; it is simple for both of them to have jobs. However, when there is a child, this shift of emphasis is much more complicated, and the child becomes living evidence of the dissatisfaction in the relationship. One woman's experience:

"We had been arguing for months. I was sure he was fooling around. I constantly accused him but he passed it off as a joke. When he did this, I pestered him about it even more, but he just ignored me or made more jokes. It nearly drove me nuts. I nagged him all the time. He finally began to get fed up with it and told me to fuck off; he even smacked me around a couple of times. But he didn't admit a thing: It was all childish and crazy but I couldn't help myself, and the more I bore down, the worse things got between us. All this wasn't doing Patrick anything but harm, he was nearly eight and he sensed the strain. He started bedwetting again and even stammering. His teacher said he was nervous in school. Maybe that woke me up, woke both of us up. Not only was our marriage troubled, but we were creating a toxic home life for our son. I decided to consult with a social worker acquaintance, and as a result my husband and I became convinced that we should all go into family therapy."

An aspect of arguing in front of a child that involves an issue of infidelity may go beyond unsettling the child's sense of security. Social scientists found that children who have grown up in a household where there has been infidelity may be more likely to carry that pattern into their own lives when they form a primary relationship. According to Brown (2001), infidelity is linked to family patterns. Parental infidelity serves as a model for the children. Thus, children whose parents engaged in infidelity are more likely to engage in infidelity themselves (Platt et al., 2008).

The dynamic involves the child identifying with the parent who has engaged in the infidelity, or the child may engage in avoidance behaviors in relationships based on the patterns the child learned from observing the parents interaction. These avoidance behaviors may result in the adult child engaging in infidelity as a way of keeping some distance from his partner. What's more, the conflicts being played out result in a decrease in the amount of support parents give to their child, which is likely to impact the parent-child relationship and tends to lead to a disruption in the child's ability to form a secure attachment (Platt et al., 2008).

GAMES NOBODY WINS

Not surprisingly, the consequences associated with infidelity extend beyond the intimate partner dyad. The prevalence of infidelity is at issue given its link to numerous deleterious outcomes. Interpersonal conflict, family disruption, violence, psychological distress (Amato & Hohmann-Marriott, 2007; Cano & O'Leary, 2000; Lusterman, 2005; Scheinkman, 2005), are all consequences of infidelity and impact a child's sense of security. As Wardle (2003, p. 127) contends, "Infidelity robs children of childhood and the joys of completely trusting the most important authority figures in their lives."

The presence of children in an unstable relationship does not mean that successful resolutions are out of reach, but it certainly does complicate things, particularly if parents resort to misusing their children as weapons in the adult conflict. Clinical experience suggests that when infidelity results in (or contributes to) relationship discord, some partners not only blame each other explicitly for the failure in their relationship but implicitly involve their children.

Instead of turning toward their partner, individuals may turn to their children, relatives, and friends for support and to make sense of the infidelity (Olson et al., 2002). For example, one parent may favor one child and the other parent another; sometimes they bid for the same offspring and the child may end up feeling like God's special gift to the world. An affair-involved father up to his ears in debt who shells out for a new car for his teenage son, saying "I owe it to him," may be involved in this ploy, as is the affair-involved mother who wears her threadbare coat for another winter so that her daughter can buy that new dress she simply must have.

On the other hand, a child's life may be made extremely miserable because his parents are competing to find fault with him or her (the "fault" allegedly "inherited" from the other spouse). This strategy is a favorite way of getting at the partner who is more sensitive to the child's needs, which is one reason why it is dangerous in a distressed relationship for a child to be a favorite of one parent. This invites misuse of the child as a weapon. In extreme situations, it may even result in physical cruelties. In any case, the child is apt to suffer emotionally either through overindulgence of his or her whims or severe deprivation. The conclusion is likely to be the child's loss of respect for the parents and a perpetuation of infantile behavior. Moreover, the parents' chances of reconciling an adultery issue are redirected and likely to be greatly diminished.

Susan Carter is a high-level executive for a woman's-wear manufacturer. She travels a good deal and her husband resents both her success and her "freedom" feeds his suspicion. As a strategy against his wife, Mr. Carter began to pamper their only child. He wanted to alienate the youngster from his mother in order to persuade her to give up her career and "stay closer to home." Of course, the hidden issue is whom is she sleeping with on her trips?

He: (disgusted) You're not doing your part. Jeremy is being neglected.

She: (angry) You're crazy!

He: (righteously) What do you mean crazy? You're never around to take care of him. You're always running off.

She: (insistent) Jeremy gets excellent care. Since when did you become father of the year?

He: (accusing) How many nights have you been gone, doing who the hell knows what, and Jeremy woke up and I had to take him into our bed!

She: (counterattacking) Why the hell are you taking a five-year-old into our bed? Jeremy is well aware of my job and shouldn't ordinarily have any difficulty with it. Are you forgetting the times he has come to work with me and gone on trips with me? What about that? What about the time I spend with him explaining how I always come back? What are you trying to create?

He: (angry) I don't like it, goddamn it!

She: (accusing) That's it! It's you who has the problem. You resent me having an independent life. Your male ego's threatened!

Eventually Mr. Carter's destructive strategy succeeded to the point where Jeremy recoiled from his mother when she returned from her business trips. The Carters were divorced a year later and Mrs. Carter moved in with a traveling colleague a week after the divorce was granted.

Another common form of triangulating children into adult dynamics occurs when a mate's authority and power is undermined. A mother may do this by subtly or not so subtly encouraging or assisting the children to break the rules established by their father who she finds too flirty with other women. For example, as the father backs down the driveway, he notices the children's toys in his path. He gets out of his car, throws the bicycles, baseball bats, trucks, and skates out of the way, dashes into the house, and shouts, "Goddamn it, Gail, have the kids keep the driveway clear. They have plenty of room to play all over the place. The driveway is off limits!"

That night, returning from work, he hears the crunch of toys under the car wheels as he pulls into the driveway. Storming into the house, he finds the family at the dinner table. Repeating the morning scene, he screams, "Who the hell left the toys in the driveway! How many times . . ."

Gail, looking relaxed and unhurried, replies coyly, "John, it's probably my fault. I was on the phone with Joan Edwards, you remember her, the one you found so attractive at the Smith's party last week, and I completely forgot about talking to the children." John turns, slams the door behind him, and closes the first act of "I'll Get You."

A related ploy for expressing hostility to a mate regarding an underlying infidelity is "Victim Villain." In one typical case, Mrs. Jackson returns from shopping late on a Saturday afternoon. Her children had been assigned to do the dishes in her absence. As she drives up to her home, she honks her horn, but nobody comes out to help with the groceries. Annoyed, she goes inside carrying one of the heavy shopping bags. There are dishes everywhere. The kitchen is a mess, nothing's been touched. Furious, she races upstairs, shuts off the blaring television, and angrily confronts her two children, aged ten and twelve. She yells, "What is the meaning of this? How could you be so inconsiderate?" At this moment, Mr. Jackson, who was reading his newspaper in the backyard appears and is requested by his wife to intercede.

In complying with his wife's request, Mr. Jackson allows his children to see that he is condescending to their mother. He implies, "My heart isn't really in this, but I'd better say these things to get your mother off our backs." In admonishing the children, he manages to uphold his image as fellow victim and adds to their mother's image as villain. He is widening the gap between himself and his partner and between her and the children—all in the service of his unspoken suspicion of her infidelity.

The emphasis here is not only the indirect form both "I'll Get You" and "Victim-Villain" take but examples of how infidelity is sometimes an underground factor that plays out through the children rather than talked out behind closed doors. The issue is not parental disagreement about the children's behavior. It is about an issue that both partners are struggling with but one that neither is ready to broach directly.

Of course, important family decisions concerning children are best made jointly by mothers and fathers; an authentic united front makes excellent sense because it gives children clear-cut direction to follow or rebel against. On more trivial issues, parental agreement is not critical. Nevertheless, the aforementioned behavior is the result of a hidden agenda and to focus on parenting techniques would be to miss the point. The critical issue here is underlying hostility communicated to a mate through the children, to everyone's detriment.

Jim and Martha O'Neill's fight about their children that turns out not to be about children at all may provide additional clarification:

She:	You're too soft on the kids. You can't just let them do whatever they want.
He:	I don't know what you're talking about. I simply told Bobby I'd rather he didn't go over to his friend's house. I didn't insist and he decided to go anyway, is that a crime?
She:	That's not the point. It's because you didn't insist that I have to take all the responsibility for the kids. Who disciplines them, me!
He:	I don't agree. I do my part. What the hell is bugging you?
She:	(angry) You're driving me crazy! I do all the dirty work. You prance through life without a care in the world. What is this? If you're not going to be home half the time, the least you can do is face up to your responsibilities when you're here.
Therapist:	Martha, it sounds as if you're angry because Jim is out so many evenings.
She:	(very red in the face) No, that's not it! It's just that he doesn't back me up when it comes to the kids.
He:	(interrupting) You're angry because the kids and I have such a good relationship. You're always trying to make me the "heavy."
She:	Oh, bull!
He:	I take enough responsibility just trying to earn a living. I think I deal with the kids just fine.
She:	How do you know how well you deal with them? You're away so much of the time, you hardly see them.
Therapist:	You know, Martha, Jim's being away so much really does seem to be bugging you. Is there something you want to say to him about that?
She:	(becoming red in the face again) No. It's just that (beginning to cry) It's just that...
He:	(uncomfortable, interrupting again) Come on, let's forget this, we're not getting anywhere.

The O'Neills thought they were battling about parental authority, "doing a good job of raising the kids," and the role of the "man of the house" but these proved to be superficial issues camouflaging more intimate ones that neither dared confront. It emerged that Martha suspected Jim was having an affair. Her suspicions arose because in recent months he was away from home more than usual, and when he returned, he did not make love to her as passionately as in the past. In later therapy sessions, Martha learned to level about her real feelings, wants, and expectations. The issue of disciplining the children never came up again, but her fears about Jim's affair did, and were supported.

Yet, another tactic for wreaking psychological havoc is employed by the parent who makes pointed or allusive remarks about the unfaithful person's behavior in the presence of the children. This usually produces embarrassment and guilt in the affair-involved parent and is quite unsettling to the children. Often the accusation is delivered in the heat of battle—"Don't give me that 'control yourself' crap! Why don't you control yourself with your girlfriend!"

The rationalization here is, "It's better for the children to know. It's time to be honest!" But, of course, this type of honesty is more a form of revenge and is likely to put the children in the center of a game of "Charge and Counter-charge." Also under the guise of being "open with the children" one parent is covertly pleading, "poor me."

Margaret, a fourteen-year-old, describes her experience with this maneuver: "My parents seem to be always fighting. They fight over the most ridiculous things. Sometimes, when they're both home, I go to a friend's house just to get some peace and quiet. . . . Last Saturday my father suggested we take a ride to the beach. Just me and him. When we got there, we walked around a little, and then we sat and talked. He told me how my mother's always running around with other men and how she is immoral and all that stuff. He said he tries very hard to be a good partner and a good father but that my mother makes things hard. I was so embarrassed and uncomfortable. I didn't know what to say so I just sat there frozen. I didn't say anything to my mother, but a couple of days later, she started to talk to me and she said the same things about him! She said she tries to make us a decent home but my father is insecure and has to prove himself with all the young women. It was disgusting. I felt so alone."

Dr. George Bach in his valuable book, *The Intimate Enemy*, adds to and summarizes the roles children may play in the marital conflict: Kids can be, and often are used as:

1. **Targets.** This occurs when parents shift the brunt of their adult battles to their child.

2. **Mediators.** As when the father says, "Tell Mommy she's acting badly."

3. **Spies.** The mother says, "Check out your father's mood."

4. **Messengers**. The mother says, "Tell your father that I'd consider reconciling, but make sure he thinks it's your idea."

5. **District attorneys**. The mother says, "I can't stand your father. But I'll stick with him because of you."

6. **Translators**. The child says, "Daddy didn't mean that. What he meant was . . ."

7. **Monitors**. The child says, "Mom didn't say that. What she said was . . ."

8. **Referees**. The child says, "Now it should be mom's chance to talk."

9. **Cupids**. Dad is really nice, you should love him.

10. **Audiences** at adult fights.

Dr. Bach goes on to say that when it comes to marital discord, all of these roles involve the child in adult issues and they should not be drawn in.

CHILDREN'S GAMES

As a refuge from their own emotional distress in an unstable family, especially one where indirect (or direct) accusations about infidelity occur and shake a child's sense of security, children develop defensive games. Their behavior is an effort to divert attention from parental conflict and on to themselves, all in the desperate service of stabilizing their home life. In short, children's games spring from the need to survive emotionally.

One such game is, "That Will Teach You!" As in all manipulative strategies, the details of "That Will Teach You!" differ according to the methods of dealing with parents that children have found most effective; usually effectiveness is a direct consequence of the weaknesses of a particular parent. For example, a boy who knows his mother is proud of a clean house will continually leave his room in a state of chaos. A girl aware of her mother's concern for what the neighbors think will carry on a loud, revealing argument in public. A son will flaunt long hair and bare feet in his conservative father's face.

While it does not deal with infidelity, a rather dramatic example of how children may involve themselves in parental dissention has been described by Joanne and Lew Koch (1976) in their book, *The Marriage Savers*. Psychiatrist Michael Soloman treated Ruth, a seven-year-old with symptoms of serious asthma. Dr. Soloman suspected that Ruth's asthma was related to family problems and decided to approach her condition by way of family therapy. Every time Dr. Soloman got close to some of the real problems in the family, the child would get sick and threaten to die.

After he had worked with the family for nearly a year, focusing on the parents' relationship, Ruth said, "I think that I should be sick for the rest of my life." The mother said, "Why in the world would you say something like that?" This seven-year-old child answered, "I've figured out that when I'm sick, the two of you know what to do, and when I'm not, the two of you don't know what to do. If I'm sick, you don't fight. If I'm not sick, you fight."

When Ruth's parents' relationship improved, so did her asthma. Dr. Soloman reports that Ruth had not been hospitalized or even seriously ill for three years following family therapy.

When children consistently play destructive emotional games, it is often because their basic trust in their parents' ability to love and care for them has been undermined, and they believe they can only get the love and care they want through manipulation. Such children opt for attention even if it is negative. This yearning for attention that finds its expression in "impossible" behavior will diminish when parents provide a firmer feeling of love and security for the children—for that an underlying trust issue like a trust breach must be addressed and resolved—without the children as audience.

TO FIGHT OR NOT TO FIGHT

Children frequently become upset by parental anger and fighting. Moreover, they often feel themselves to be the cause of parental conflict. This is particularly true of the chronically angry family where fights don't get at the heart of an issue; consequently, there is a vague instability that results in a child's anxiety. Given these realities, would it be best to spare the children this emotional burden by not allowing them to witness or be involved in parental discord? Many parents respond affirmatively and with some justification. First, there are times when the issues being discussed or argued, such as infidelity are too sensitive and therefore inappropriate for young witnesses.

Second, and more important, parents who regularly tear each other apart in front of their children in scenes reminiscent of *Who's Afraid of Virginia Woolf?* are creating a very poor relationship model for their offspring. These are tactics to be aware of and guarded against. The continuance of destructive interaction is an indication that professional intervention is warranted. Without intervention, far too many children are likely to grow up thinking that a committed relationship is an excessively troublesome and painful arrangement. What's more, if a serious trust issue is aired in front of the children or if it is alluded to, a child's view of relationships, as we've seen is distorted; the child is more likely to repeat that pattern in his or her adult relationship.

Considering the disadvantages, parents can decide not to argue in front of the children. However, simply not arguing in front of the children is a poor solution. Not only is it a virtual impossibility to have fights that the children won't become aware of, but a lack of open discussion actually robs the children of potential benefit. The one critical guideline is: Keep the fighting aboveboard and resolution-oriented. Parental fighting in which both partners stay with the issues and do not resort to crude, manipulative strategies actually helps prepare children for their own future inevitable relationship disagreements.

Marsha is a slim thirty-one-year-old woman with long black hair and dark, searching eyes. She recently graduated from the City College of New York and works part time as a laboratory technologist. Marsha has been married for six years; she and her husband Richard, who also works on a part-time basis, share the rearing of their two children. Marsha describes her parents' marriage:

"They fought a lot of the time. You could hear them four blocks away, but I think they were basically happy. I remember many of their fights being followed by a resolution, a making up. They said things to each other in anger that they apologized for. They always made sure I was aware of the apologies. When they got mad at me, I was told, 'Being angry doesn't mean I don't love you.' When they were mad at each other, I was reminded of the same thing— 'We may disagree about some things and feel very angry but that doesn't mean we hate each other.' They taught me that a person may not like something about you but still like you. This is a lesson that's made a critical difference in my life. Rejection, for instance, isn't as traumatic to me as it is to many people. I know on an emotional level that I can't be liked by everyone. Rejection doesn't make me feel worthless. Another thing, I believe I am probably more assertive than most women. Being wrong and possibly incurring somebody's wrath doesn't frighten me. I've seen wrath and it's not so terrible."

Richard comments: "I like Martha's folks very much, and I agree with her view of their impact on her. I think she was very fortunate to grow up in a household where people didn't believe in facades. Her parents don't display only their best side. They are very real. My parents, on the other hand, should have censored themselves. Their fights scared me. The accusations of affairs, his and hers embarrassed me and left me with an apprehension about fighting— you never know what is going to be said and some things once said can never be erased. Even when they weren't actually fighting they were indirectly hostile to each other. I picked up a lot of bad habits. First of all, I didn't speak up when something bothered me. I would sit and stew. When I did say something, it was aimed at provoking guilt in the other person, just the way my parents did with each other. I tried to get my way by using emotional blackmail. I also had to work out the trust issues I came into our relationship with. It's only in the last year or so that I have learned, mostly through Marsha's example, to speak up and say what I want and what's bothering me. No camouflaging. No beating around the bush and no hitting below the belt."

It may come down to this: To the extent that unexpressive or passive parents wean themselves from the notion that peace and quiet must reign, they will have moved to a starting position for conflict resolution. This is possible without undue harm to their children. In contrast, those partners who are chronically angry are probably banging away at the wrong issues and would best consider their posture in light of its potential damage to their children.

Most important, fair fighting, that is, fighting in which both partners are honestly striving to resolve a conflict rather than to destroy an opponent can comfortably take place in front of the children. Ideally, children will learn by example to fight for their wants and express their feelings constructively. Naturally, some issues (e.g., extra-relationship sex) are best aired privately. Airing adult issues like infidelity or other serious trust issues with children as witnesses is not only poor judgment, as the research notes it has a deleterious impact on children that is likely to carry into their adult relationships.

Dirty, underhanded fighting is best done secretly. However, if this is the best level of fighting a couple can attain, they should consider professional assistance. A couple can tell if they fight poorly by the results—one or both partners are constantly hurt and conflicts are hardly ever resolved. Issues involving the children that are fought and refought but resist resolution despite compromise should be reconsidered.

What if the children were not the issue, would another issue surface? If so, discuss it and see where it leads. Even under the best of circumstances, manipulative emotional games will sometimes be played, but as side events, not center-stage attractions. As parents become more aware of and are able to express their own feelings and their children's real needs, games of manipulation will yield to healthy and open communication.

Last, research reported in *Journal of Consulting and Clinical Psychology* (Gottman, 1993) suggests that couples who report solid relationships actually disagree more than those who are less satisfied with the relationship. The critical difference is how they disagree and exiting before the disagreement goes south. Disagreeing isn't the problem, how the disagreement is approached is the critical factor.

AVOIDING TRIANGULATING CHILDREN INTO ADULT CONFLICTS

Triangulating, as we have seen, is the tactic of drawing another person into an issue that the person is peripheral to. Next, guidelines for avoiding this all-too-common, but ineffective and issue-worsening tactic (Block & Bartell, 2002):

1. **If you are having difficulty with a family member, direct your energy toward resolution with that family member.** Avoid deflecting your focus to someone else within the family (particularly a child). If you are discouraged because you have tried settling things and all your efforts have been unsuccessful, consult with a

professional outside the immediate family for expert advice on how to move forward effectively.

2. **Honestly consider the patterns of interaction with your children.** The power of awareness is often underestimated. Once we identify a pattern, we can change it. Merely identifying a pattern often involves a change of attitude—in order to see it, a parent has to be open to the likelihood that he or she is a contributor. This admission may be difficult, but it is well worth it; attitudes and actions must change together to correct troublesome communication.

3. **Stay calm.** When you are distressed, it is particularly tempting to draw children in as allies or pawns to avenge and temporarily alleviate your feelings. Since underlying anxiety drives triangles, staying calm in the face of pressure to triangulate is particularly important. A calm individual can be an effective antidote to family anxiety and can help ease the resistance to change.

4. **Self-soothe.** The key to staying calm is learning how to soothe yourself. As noted earlier, self-soothing involves turning inward and accessing your own resources to regain your emotional balance. It is the ability to comfort and care for yourself without self-indulgence. It does not involve tantrums; whining; self-pity; or bingeing on food, drink, or drugs. It does involve taking care of yourself while you're not getting along with your partner. Self-soothing permits you to quiet and calm yourself. The process requires that you not give up on yourself, not tell yourself it is too hard to settle your emotions. It may be hard not to draw in the children—especially if that has been the pattern—but not too hard. You have to stick with yourself, just as you would with a friend going through a difficult time.

5. **If you can't settle your emotions, control your behavior.** Behave in a productive manner that you'll respect afterward, even if your emotions suggest otherwise. In other words, ask yourself, "If I felt better, how would I handle this?" Then do your best to approximate that behavior. In contrast, when you start saying, "Maybe I shouldn't do this, but . . ." or "Maybe I shouldn't say this but . . ." take your own advice!

6. **Do not promote or collaborate with family secrets.** Secrets, whether they are subtly conveyed with a wink, or obvious and blatant, are a sure sign of a triangle. Those secrets that are agreed upon implicitly may take the form of simply not informing a spouse about something pertinent that occurred with a child. The child is aware that you are keeping information from the other parent but neither of you have explicitly agreed on the secret. In contrast, the obvious and blatant form occurs when either a child or a parent initiates the secret: "Don't tell Dad I got suspended from school, he'll just go ballistic and it will end up in a whole family mess." Or, "I won't tell your dad you were arrested for shoplifting, it would only break his heart, and then he'll break your neck."

7. **Do not use a child (regardless of age) as a confidant.** This is especially important when it comes to issues in the family. For example, trying to protect children by telling them what is wrong with the other parent may have good intentions but creates an alignment with the "good" parent and will likely alienate the "problem" parent. Telling a child your view of the problems in your relationship is definitely a poor idea. Putting children in the position of siding with your perspective of the other parent's problems or the relationship conflicts places an unfair burden on them. Children should not have to choose sides between their parents. They

need to discover their own truths without your influence. That is part of family life. The only exception to this is the instance where a parent is a danger to a young child.

8. **Change first.** While it is easier and more productive when relationship partners work together to change, either one may rein in his or her contributions and thereby disrupt a negative pattern. Either partner can initiate a discussion of the parenting issues that emphasizes concern and offers solutions rather than blame and bitterness.

9. **Consider that we all inherit the unsolved problems of our past.** That is, whatever is occurring with us in our family can be traced to the struggles of our childhood family. For example, the parent who is overprotective would be wise to look at his or her own upbringing. What is it in that upbringing that bears on your behavior in your present family? Of course, the same look backward is warranted for any problematic pattern in our present family. If we do not take this into consideration, we are more likely to repeat past patterns or negatively rebel against them.

10. **Keep the lines of communication open in the family.** While allying yourself with one of the children or talking to them about issues that should remain between spouses is off-limits, appropriate discussion is not. In fact, just the opposite is true. Children are very perceptive, and it would be a disservice to them to deny that anything is wrong. However, rather than casting blame on the other parent, a statement that validates the child's perception without taking sides is warranted. For example, "It's true, Dad and I are working out some differences and sometimes it is a little rough." This states what is going on without casting blame. Of course, a parent may, at times, be "invited" to cast blame: "Mom, I think Dad is a real jerk for yelling at you. . . ." Although it is very tempting to go along with that type of statement, especially when you are feeling upset, it is not helpful to the child. An effective response puts the "invitation" back to the adults involved: "Honey, I am feeling upset with your father right now, but it is my job to work that out with him, not yours. Your job is to work out the best relationship with me and your dad that you can have."

Sound Thinking and Smart Moves

1. While an affair is usually akin to a head-on collision, if a couple work out the emotional issues in a healthy manner children may actually benefit. They benefit from parents who show them how a conscious and loving couple can grow together, through good times and bad.

2. What to say to children about a parent's infidelity: the younger the children are, the less a parent needs to say about it. If the children have heard or suspect something is wrong, and are asking questions, it is very important to recognize that a factual, discrete—rather than emotional—response is needed, it does not have to involve details. It is worse for children to feel there are secrets being withheld from them, especially when these secrets are affecting them. When they have no idea about what has happened, there is no reason to tell them.

3. When children are aware of a breach of trust from the people they depend on (their parents), their ability to trust others can be seriously impaired. They may be overly

suspicious, emotionally distant, or refrain from committing to a relationship because they can't trust the other person will act honorably and be there for them. If this is a concern, and it definitely should be, this suggests parents not only should correct the model they are presenting but have conversations about trust with their children. Otherwise, the children may avoid being hurt in the same way they witnessed a parent being hurt by keeping emotionally distant from others.

Chapter 8

GETTING OUT: DIVORCE AND SEPARATION

THE AGONIZING SHOWDOWN

The prevalence of infidelity is often an emotional wound that has links to numerous negative outcomes, including interpersonal conflict, family disruption, violence, distress, and disruption of children's lives (Cano & O'Leary, 2000). What's more, divorcing a long-time partner for some is a loss that may be greater than the loss of a relative (Hooyman & Kramer, 2008). Indeed, losing someone through divorce or separation can be experienced as similar to losing a part of one's self and may resonate for years (Hooyman & Kramer, 2008). Hooyman and Kramer in their research note that when divorce occurs, multiple losses follow. The secondary losses include friends, income, and in-laws; in addition, the breakup may awaken feelings from losses during childhood.

Added to the consequences of infidelity, divorce rates are significantly higher among couples who have experienced infidelity. A recent analysis of three clinical infidelity studies conducted by Marín et al. (2014) revealed that 53 percent of infidelity cases ended in divorce within five years of couples therapy, compared with 23 percent of cases of couples therapy where infidelity was not reported. What's more, a study that investigated the perceived reasons for parental divorce and attachment styles found that adult children who perceived extra-relationship affairs and expressions of overt anger as reasons for the divorce were more likely to have an insecure attachment style (Walker & Ehrenberg, 1998). In short, they developed their own relationship difficulties.

While some studies conclude that an affair has a high likelihood of ending a relationship, certainly, all relationships scarred by infidelity do not end with divorce (Chamy & Pamass, 1995). However, most of the studies about consequences of infidelity find negative outcomes like rage, broken trust, decreased personal and sexual confidence, damaged self-esteem, and fear of abandonment as well as a surge of justification to leave the affair-involved partner (Chamy & Pamass, 1995).

Interestingly, other teams of researchers concluded that partners who divorce because of their spouse's infidelity experienced less depression than those who end their relationship for other reasons (Spanier & Margolis 1983; Sweeney & Horowitz 2001). Further, men and women face different adaptive problems related to various types of infidelity and are more likely to have different reactions to partner's infidelity. It is more difficult for men to forgive a sexual infidelity than an emotional infidelity and they are more likely to end a current relationship following a partner's sexual infidelity. Women, in contrast, tend to be more impacted by a partner's emotionally involved affair, even if sex is not part of it (Shackelford et al., 2002).

The urge to destroy the sexual wanderer sometimes becomes overwhelming for both men and women. Even in an unhappy relationship, divorce is a grim prospect involving the breakup of the home and the division of property, the fierce struggle to win over the children, the disruption of friendships, and the harsh financial penalty that may be exacted of the adulterer.

The aggrieved spouse's lawyer is likely to make the road to divorce quite rocky, advising the affair-involved adversary to settle generously out of court since in some cases the judge may be biased against an adulterer. The consequences of divorce are frequently hard on the punisher as well—financial ruin, embarrassment, and the breakup of the family. For a couple with children, divorce ends the marriage but not their mutual involvement; since the children are a link that neither remarriage nor absence can break. Rather than being a final settlement, the divorce becomes an adjustment the family has to adapt itself to, a process that may take several years.

Peggy Quinn is an attractive woman with style and grace. During the fifteen years she was married to Ed, she thought they had a good marriage. But now, four years after her divorce, she recalls that during the last five years of the marriage, she and her husband only slept together once or twice a month, usually after Ed had had a few drinks. Peggy accepted their deteriorating sex life as the inevitable consequence of many years together until one of her "kind" friends told her that Ed's pleasures and interests lay elsewhere. The weeks that followed were such agony for both that even before divorce proceedings were under way, Ed moved out. Peggy, suddenly swamped by the technicalities of living, felt lost. Not only did she have the responsibility for two children, food, and clothing, but for financial records and transactions that her husband had usually managed. In Peggy's words:

"The problems of starting over were unanticipated. It was extremely difficult returning to the job market after a ten-year absence, but it became necessary due to the increased expenses of a split household. I was unprepared for the attitude society still had toward a divorced woman and how difficult it was to get credit. So-called friends dropped me socially. It was as if they thought it was not safe for me to be in the presence of their husbands. Do people think divorce is contagious? The loneliness was horrid; hours on the phone or sitting in front of the television were a poor substitute for a mate. I had had most of the responsibility of child rearing and taking care of the house before the separation and divorce, but these tasks became much more tiring, meaningless, and thankless after working all day. I got very down sometimes thinking that now I was breadwinner, father as well as mother, housekeeper, laundress, ad infinitum. When my youngest developed medical problems, I had to take the major responsibility. Eventually she required surgery. At one point, I became almost suicidal under the pressure."

Children and money were the two binding agents that forced Peggy and Ed to continue seeing each other. These confrontations were very delicate and painful. When a man and woman have lived together for many years, the connective tissue—emotional attachment—does not dissolve so easily. A tone of voice, a gesture, a certain comment can twist a knife in either the rejecter or the rejected. Peggy continues:

"The bitterness between Ed and me ran deep. The chill in each other's presence was devastating. It was several years before we were able to treat each other casually and lightly. For me, the process was filled with self-pity and hate. The thought that he had a lover waiting in the wings for the final decree drove me wild. When I thought of him with her, I became unsettled. All that we had worked for, he was making a good living; we had grown up together; I sacrificed, he sacrificed; now she, rather than I, savors the rewards of those difficult years. I couldn't accept the injustice! I was consumed with getting back. I thought of turning him in to the IRS for tax fraud. I considered blackmail, disfigurement, murder. I settled for giving him a hard time with the kids. I turned them against him by presenting an image of him as a bum; I made it hard for him to see them; I tortured him through them.

"Slowly, I calmed down and started to dream of a new life. This began about three years after the divorce. There were still hassles between us and awkward moments, but things were becoming reasonably civilized. I began to exercise, take care of my appearance; I started therapy, school, and dance lessons. It wasn't my intention to distract myself nor was it to lessen the ache. By this time it was already muted; it was about bringing back my nerve. I was determined to face the world not as Peggy Quinn, amputated from Ed Quinn, but as a whole human being. I had run out of pity. Out of a long period of submergence in my marriage and the agonizing period of discontent followed by my continuing struggle, I am discovering something very important: me!"

Divorce need not be the signal that life is stopped and is never to be resumed. Peggy Quinn survived and eventually prospered. Many others, men, women, and children have likewise succeeded in the face of broken relationships. Sadly, though, the process is typically characterized by animosity, revenge, retribution, and bitterness, especially if one of the partners has a lover. Although such involvements are frequent, they are seldom the only basis of divorce; rather they tend to be the catalyst in the destruction of an unsatisfactory marriage. This is difficult for some people to accept. To most of the Quinns's friends, the affair was held solely responsible for splitting up a "beautiful couple."

Today, almost everyone has heard of a relationship split that seemed sudden and unexpected. Of course, this is rarely the case and a closer look at the Quinns's relationship reveals not fulfillment marred by a brief bout with lust but a profound unhappiness resembling that of the characters in Elia Kazan's novel, *The Arrangement*. In this story, the protagonist has become increasingly dissatisfied with his marriage and at forty-three engages in a serious affair with a younger woman. He is confused by his behavior and feels guilty because he either doesn't understand or won't acknowledge that his wife's good nature is leaving him unfulfilled and conflicted. His wife, true to her helping nature, arranges a plan, a different "style of life" for the two of them, with the hope it will draw them together and rid her husband of his misery.

The husband complies out of passivity or sheer exhaustion, and for almost a year, they live in a way designed to protect the couple (him!) from the material and carnal desires that threaten their illusory togetherness. The arrangement, appropriately called the "fortress," backfires: instead of just eliminating the husband's lustful desires for other women, it causes him to become passive and impotent.

During the eleven-month fortress period, the husband and wife are the envy of all their friends. The wife's emphasis on the "pure" life and the husband's surface responsiveness project an image of sharing, togetherness, and unusual devotion. Below the surface, however, is serious conflict, for the dream of "happily ever after" is not shared; it belongs only to the wife. A near-fatal auto accident, which is recognized by the husband as a suicidal gesture, forcefully shatters the togetherness fantasy. The husband, after his recovery, leaves his wife.

Perhaps with less drama, but through an essentially similar process, Ed and Peggy Quinn's marriage dissolved. Although this couple appeared to share common goals, their "arrangement" was based on one person's dream. The other was silently off in a different direction. The affair that triggered the divorce was the fierce blow that knocked down the fortress.

There are occasions when divorce is more directly the result of an adulterous relationship. In these instances, it is the deceived mate's overreaction and the adulterous mate's guilt and defensiveness that bring the relationship to a halt. Thus, what may have started as a casual episode for a person contented with his or her marriage but flattered by attention from the opposite sex is transformed into a divorce.

Friends may speed the movement toward divorce by taking sides and reinforcing the deceived mate's feelings of injustice and hurt, and the adulterer's sense of guilt. ("Haven't you hurt her/him enough already?") However gratifying it may be to receive the support of friends, it sometimes does more harm than good. Yet the emotional damage one experiences after discovering a husband or wife is having an affair makes one crave this type of loyalty from friends. There is nothing sweeter than hearing a husband called a total bastard for cheating on his lovely wife with some "call girl," or a wife denounced as an "ungrateful bitch" who doesn't deserve her hardworking husband.

Such denunciations help to polarize the couple and interfere with their efforts to communicate and sensibly sort out their situation. This is not to say that discussion of sensitive issues with friends is best avoided. At times of crisis, friendship is especially valuable. However, caution is suggested in following the advice of a friend who may be too emotionally involved and biased to be helpful in the long run.

FALSE ALARMS

Although divorce motivated exclusively by adultery is not common, it is not uncommon for an individual to threaten divorce in an effort to keep a spouse in line. One wife who likes to show her husband that she is not to be taken for granted, and at the same time make sure that he is as fully committed to her as ever stages a mock divorce ritual every few months by dramatically packing her bags, all the while screaming her complaints in a furious tirade. Each time as she starts phoning for a hotel reservation, her husband concedes.

In this household, the false alarm serves as a jolting reminder to the husband that his wife feels strongly about his extramarital behavior and it works—temporarily. Too often partners who either threaten divorce or storm out of the house or isolate themselves in a hotel find that the payoff is disappointing:

"This was the second time I had discovered his infidelities. That was it! I told him he'd had it and I left. At first, I felt really great. I felt very much in control. I had a regal room in a luxury hotel. After all, I thought, if I'm going to leave, there's no use punishing myself. I might as well treat myself well. I ordered a dinner of prime ribs and a whiskey sour from room service and felt very much protected in this environment. In the morning, I ordered eggs Benedict, showered, and luxuriated in bed reading a copy of Mademoiselle I had sent up. I didn't feel angry at all; that had seeped out of me when I left my husband pleading with me to remain home.

"All this time I hadn't left my hotel room. The next afternoon, though, I decided to put on a nice outfit and go down for lunch. I sat at a little table in the hotel cafe and ordered a sandwich and a drink. I didn't feel terribly comfortable sitting there myself. As a matter of fact, I was damned uncomfortable. In contrast to my room, which felt safe, the place was large, austere, and impersonal. I imagined it as a refuge for the disconnected and lonely. I didn't like the idea of being part of this. After a while, a man approached my table and asked to join me. He looked decent enough and seemed simply to want conversation and company, but I got scared stiff and retreated to my room.

"That evening I really began to worry. I'd figured all along that I would go home again, but now I wondered if my husband had seen my leaving as final and whether he would be there when I arrived. Even if he was, would he be receptive? Would he make the first move? If he didn't, would I be able to? All these things began to trouble me, so I decided to call. I spoke to my teenage son and said, 'I just called to let you know that your father and I had a bad fight and I left. I wanted you to know where I am.' As I hoped, my son told my husband where I was, and he was at the hotel soon after with an apology. He promised to behave himself and we left for home together."

Certainly not everyone who temporarily leaves a mate suffers the high separation anxiety this woman experienced. Sometimes a respite from each other is a very useful experience for a couple: it offers an opportunity to function independently and to assess areas of overdependence; for some people, it provides a very important "cooling off" or "time-out" period. The difficulty lies not so much in the separation but in how it is used. Often, rather than employing a brief separation constructively, a spouse is attempting to get back, to "teach the son of a bitch a lesson," and leaving then becomes a form of punishment.

Predictably, after the punishment is administered, an emotional but superficial peace pact is drawn up. "You're right," one spouse may say to the other in a disarmingly nondefensive manner. "Forgive me, it won't happen again. Promise." At this point, the issue is likely to be neatly tucked away. The pattern is outburst—withdrawal—illusory resolution. It is as if both husband and wife silently consent to leave well enough alone.

This pattern is most popular not only in some instances of adultery, but with compulsive gamblers, alcoholics, and emotionally troubled individuals married to "rescuers." It is also a factor with couples who have a shaky relationship that one or both fear to breakup. Unless the difficulties are discussed thoroughly and real issues are resolved, the pattern is likely to be repeated and become increasingly corrosive to both partners.

TO DIVORCE OR NOT

When is a committed relationship not working? When should one seek a divorce? An easily applied guideline to answer these questions does not exist because marriage and other long-term relationships is much too complex a process to fit specific formulas. Some general observations, however, may apply: A relationship is not working when you feel that you can function better without your spouse than with him or her. It is not working when you would rather be alone or with somebody else than with your partner, not sometimes but usually. It is not working when you think your children would profit from the absence of your spouse. He or she is abusing the children in some way, or there is chronic and underhanded arguing that has not been resolved even with treatment. A relationship is not working when there is more unhappiness related to it than not. When, then, should a couple wisely consider divorce? In most cases, not without professional consultation.

Then, whenever it is clear that husband and wife are not functioning together without severe damage to one or both, physically or emotionally, and that the destructiveness is irreversible or reversible only with an effort that is not forthcoming from both partners.

Once it is determined that a committed relationship is not working and is unsalvageable, divorce is the best way to ensure the well-being of the partners and, especially, of the children. Youngsters are better off with divorced parents than in a subtly crazy-making family. Unfortunately, many couples caught in an irreversible and mutually destructive process do not get out. They persist, despite the lack of emotional closeness, and the consequent psychosomatic illnesses, infidelities, disturbances in their children, and general misery. Here are some of the reasons for the deadlock:

1. The one who would like to initiate the divorce feels that doing so would be an admission that he or she is wrong and that the other is right after all. Or if one decides to leave, the "deserted" partner may try to prevent the separation in order to avoid the suggestion that he or she, having been abandoned, is inferior and the spouse who left is superior. These couples remain together not out of love but out of hate. As one woman put it, "I'd leave the philandering bastard in a flash, but I'll be damned if I am going to give him the opportunity to come out of this thing a wounded hero!"

2. Each partner may want the other to assume the responsibility and guilt for the breakup. For example, neither may want to play "bad guy" or "home wrecker" in front of the children, so they stick together in order not to let the other have this advantage. Little thought is given to what such an arrangement does to the children.

3. One or both may be excessively afraid of loneliness. Most people abhor loneliness; some are terrorized to the point where being left alone makes them feel like an abandoned orphan. They marry to avoid being alone—or to be "rescued" from their parents, and once married, they cannot tolerate being alone for more than a few hours. This is like having a fear of the dark, except that it operates around the clock. Both usually

end up lonelier than before they were married. And to the loneliness is added bitterness. For each is fragile and requires constant reassurance from the other. If this is denied, the "rejected" spouse draws back and the other now feels rejected. The distance between the two quickly increases. Usually these people find it difficult to be intimate with anyone, although out of need for reassurance, they act passionate and may have had a number of affairs. They continue together, quietly destroying each other, because of a fear of being apart and alone. They do not want to face what faces them.

Aside from the psychological reasons for avoiding a divorce, there are practical factors that couples offer for continuing the relationship. Primary among these is financial circumstances. For middle-income families, the expense of two households (not to mention legal fees) presents a formidable barrier to divorce. The financial hardship, and the psychological needs discussed earlier, should be weighed against a living arrangement that slowly eats away at integrity and well-being.

LOVERS UNITED?

If a relationship is broken by an affair and the lovers do not marry or otherwise commit, the extra-relationship involvement is likely to be seen as an irresponsible fling. In contrast, the partnering of the lovers seems to provide justification for the divorce. It is then assumed that the original marriage was unhappy and that the illicit transgression was sincere and honorable. The affair becomes sanctified, and the couple can once again enter society's fold. This is the idealized version. In actual life, it is a rarity.

Morton Hunt in his study *The Affair* states that of the unfaithful people he interviewed, only about one out of ten had married, or were about to marry or fully committed to the person with whom they were having an extra-relationship affair. Regarding the interviewees in his study who were affair-involved and divorced, Hunt explains, "Only part of these divorces were sought in order to marry the partner outside; even when they were, the planned remarriages took place only about half the time."

There are many reasons why the majority of lovers do not marry or otherwise stay together after a divorce frees them to do so. For one thing, an affair resembles courtship and divorce alters this. During the affair, lovers limit themselves to a narrow behavioral and social repertoire aimed at pleasing each other. Often this repertoire consists of precisely the kind of behavior lacking at home. In addition, there is the excitement of "lovers against the world." The clandestine adventure includes secret trips, sojourns at hotels under false names, flirty texts, and so on. Their emotional investment in these risks convinces the lovers that the affair is the high point of their lives.

With the divorce, the drama calms down, and while the strains of secrecy and jealousy are removed, new ones are introduced. For example, a lover may "cop out" after being exposed to some unfamiliar and unpalatable divorce-battle behavior, his depleted finances, her ugly emotional outbursts, vindictiveness, all of which have a dampening effect on romance. Now the lovers really get to know each other and some of the revelations may be totally unexpected if not shocking.

The experience of Jeffrey Fisher provides an illustration of a downhill slide. Mr. Fisher, after separating from his wife, moved in with his mistress. For the first time in their two-year relationship, they were able to assume the roles of live-in lovers. Soon conflict appeared. Jeffrey was passionately involved in his profession. Helen demanded he be more attentive now that they were finally together. In the past, she had understood his difficulty in seeing her, he was married.

Now, she insisted, there was no excuse. If he worked late, she became upset. If he was tied up in his job for several days in a row, she was irritated, resentful, and openly antagonistic. Jeffrey, seeing this side of Helen, began to have serious misgivings about the relationship, although he had felt certain for months that he wanted to marry her. Helen, sensing the withdrawal, felt frightened and betrayed. As a result, she became more antagonistic and on many mornings provoked an argument just before Jeffrey departed for the office. Jeffrey then began to work even later, and Helen felt more left out than ever. The cycle lasted six weeks; the new marriage, conceived in idealism, died unborn.

Sometimes children complicate the picture. One man, childless, came to know his lover's children for the first time after she obtained a quick Mexican divorce. Not used to children, he became easily annoyed with them, particularly since they were demanding a great deal of attention during this difficult and confusing period. He constantly snapped at them, which only made them more demanding of attention. Their mother was in the middle. At times, she sided with him and agreed that "the children needed discipline," while on other occasions she demanded he be more tolerant of their behavior. Though she felt compelled to try to keep the children in line ("If they don't behave, he'll leave"), she hated herself for being cruel to them. Her former husband began to appear increasingly desirable, but he would have no part of her. Finally, after four months, her lover left. He walked out without explanation; there was none needed.

These are some common complications that can destroy lovers' desire to marry or continue in an unmarried but committed state, but even under more harmonious circumstances, an extra-relationship affair can falter after divorce. A harsh divorce fight hardly promotes enthusiasm for another marriage; so many new divorces suddenly find themselves reluctant to take the plunge again. Even living together without marriage may not turn into a long-term commitment.

"I met him at a party given by my publisher at the close of summer two years ago. We spent the fall and winter getting to know each other, a time which I will cherish as the most unambiguously wonderful of my life. After a long, exciting winter, we decided we wanted to try living together. He was single. I was involved in a marriage of convenience. There were no children. I left my husband despite his promise of a bitter, contested divorce battle and moved in with Eric.

"I found living with Eric sort of comfortable. It was much better than living with my husband. But I had a nagging sense of uneasiness. Once I was free, I was jumpy about getting tied down again. Eric wanted very much to get married when the divorce came through but I didn't want that. I didn't even want a full-time live-in relationship. I was feeling tied down with him. For instance, he expected me to be with him for dinner every evening and that bothered me. I don't want always to be occupied with the same person. I hadn't really explored standing on my own two feet, or other men. First there was my husband, we were married very young—then there was Eric. I wanted to chase around or be chased around a little bit. . . . I felt so pressured to make the right decision that at one point I thought of committing suicide. My fantasy of suicide, it turned out, constituted the bottom line for me. Conflict that had been burrowing within since adolescence regarding independence/ dependence, masked quite marvelously by the sacred bonds of marriage, was now out in the open. The choice became to face life by myself or spend the rest of my days angry. I decided not to commit myself to Eric. We split up and only see each other occasionally now."

When an affair that contributes to the breakup of a marriage by its promise of a fresh start fails to evolve into a new lasting relationship, is anything to be gleaned from the experience? Yes and no. Some people, particularly the pathologically insecure, the compulsively promiscuous, the highly guarded and defensive who disallow intimacy in their lives, learn little. For them, infidelity, whether it contributes to discord and eventual divorce or drones on undiscovered, is an empty experience, except perhaps for some physical joy. They bring little to a love affair and receive little from it. For others, however, the dissolution of the affair is not all pain and loss. Conversations held sometime after the expiration of both the marriage and the competing affair attest to this. From Jeffrey Fisher:

"My marriage was a disaster. It was a relationship that can only be described as consistently destructive. Unfortunately, my relationship with Helen began to be tainted with the same rigid, destructive elements that had existed in my marriage. This time, though, I was aware of what was occurring and I put a stop to it before it got out of hand. Helen and I are still friends. We didn't allow our differences to destroy us but we would never have made it together. Work is my passion and I realize that very few women are going to be willing to become a distant number two in my life. I complained viciously to my wife and to Helen that it was unfair of them not to accept my priorities. But it was equally unfair of me to demand that they change their wants and goals. Nobody was at fault. As a matter of fact, realizing this, I am on better terms with my wife and women in general than ever before. I may just be one of those people not well suited to the type of commitment marriage requires. One of these days that might change, but if not, I think I can live a reasonably satisfactory life without marriage."

And this from the woman seeking independence:

"I've learned a number of things on my own. More often than not, the learning of them has been a lonely business, but I suspect I might have been unable to grasp the point of things in any other way. I have a renewed confidence in my personal effectiveness. From daddy to husband to lover was just too much. I lived with the fear of being left empty and, more simply, of being left. It was a horrible state. I had lost the ability to think, to imagine, to feel. Being completely on my own was the only way I could claw my way back to independence. Emotionally, I am stronger for the experience. My relationship with men has an adult-relating-to-adult quality rather than the parent-child pattern I experienced in the past. I've served a much needed apprenticeship with myself. One of these days I might even try marriage again. I think I am almost ready to handle it on more mature terms. This little girl has become a woman."

But what of the extraneous sexual involvements that do evolve into a marriage? Do they confirm the romantic myth that lovers who have struggled long to possess each other live happily ever after, or do they belie it? Dr. Frank Pittman (*Private Lies*, 1989) weighed in on this question. In the study he cited, the divorce rate among those who married their lovers was 75 percent, a rate higher than that of second marriages in general. This rate of failure is considerable, especially what it cost emotionally to all involved.

Perhaps, then, there is something about the illicit origin of such relationships that dooms them: The puritan conscience would find such an answer intellectually and morally satisfying. Indeed, in a fair number of cases, there does seem to be a special kind of relationship problem or cluster of problems that relates to the way the relationship began. Trust is the foundation of a relationship and a relationship born out of an affair is likely to have an unspoken ghost whispering in times of difficulty: "Will he (or she) do to me what was done before?" Paradoxically, the issue of beginning the new relationship in a cloud of lies may be precisely what undermines the new one. There is also, noted by Hunt in his book cited previously, the loss of the excitement that the clandestine nature of the affair had provided.

Lovers united? Sometimes yes and happily. Much more often not, or yes, but unhappily. Influenced by passion, consumed by hope, giddy with love (or revenge), the recently divorced, whether "rejected" or "rejecter," would better stop, think, and wait. Going from one marriage immediately into another commitment, even if preceded by a long-term adulterous relationship, is high-risk. At a time of emotional weariness from the divorce process, the individual is least likely to exercise sound judgment. Living alone for a time, or experimenting with trial cohabitation, may improve the odds for success the second time around.

THE COPING PROCESS

There are no typical divorced people but there are emotional reactions and adjustments that are common to most divorced people. First, there are the problems of living alone. The divorced woman frequently must learn how to handle money, particularly if her husband (and before that, her father) has managed the finances. Her long-time social and economic dependence will leave her feeling bereft. She may panic, not occasionally, but frequently. Usually, she has the children, which present at once a burden and an incentive to conquer the pain.

For the man who frequently also has long-standing habits of dependence, the children and the comforts of home his wife probably provided may be sorely missed. Rights of visitation seldom compensate for daily contact with the children. Learning to cook, create a comfortable living environment, and cope directly with sundries, supermarkets, and the endless details of daily living may appear overwhelming. Rather than bother, some men resign themselves to hotels or furnished rooms that only make their lives bleaker.

Husband and wife share a complex and confusing interplay of emotions: anger, sadness, guilt, fear, relief, and excitement. The final decree is a release from the bickering, delays, recriminations, legalities, and lawyers, but sometimes the release is short-lived. A sense of failure and doubt may prevail: "Is there something wrong with me, some fatal flaw that propelled me into this circumstance? Is there someone out there with whom I will be able to form a close relationship? Am I capable of that?"

From the initial separation through (and often after) the divorce, an emotional digestion process occurs. During this time, a number of attitudes and negative emotions may burst in and out of daily experience, anger, jealousy, plots of revenge, loneliness, and panic. After a reasonable period of time, which may range from several weeks to perhaps a year or sometimes even longer, the divorce is likely to be digested. Sometimes it is not. When separated or divorced partners fail to wean themselves from each other and continue to experience intense guilt, fear, dependence, and hate, they go through life like battle casualties. They may congratulate themselves on their freedom, but psychologically they resemble zombies.

Following are some of the more common emotional and attitudinal traps that occur during and after the separation and divorce process. They are natural reactions, yet if they continue to be intense and frequent long after the divorce has been finalized, they will be serious inhibitors.

1. Stereotypic thinking. "No man can be trusted" or "All women want is your money" or "Men are only out for sex." These statements serve as protective shields. What people who make these statements are really saying is, "I have been hurt and I am scared of being hurt again; since men (women) are no good anyway, I have ample reason for avoiding them." It is this attitude, not the basic "evilness" of men or women that prevents the divorced individual from going out and meeting new people.

   If an individual does socialize but continues to see people through rigid preconceptions, a self-fulfilling prophecy is likely to occur. That is, if people are treated with suspicion and mistrust, they are likely to return in kind, confirming the divorced individual in his or her opinion that most people have something up their sleeve, are deceptive, can't be trusted, and so on.

2. Blaming. Blame is corrosive. It eats away at life, blighting the capacity for joy and intimacy. The woman who keeps calling her ex-husband an s.o.b., the husband who keeps telling his new wife or lover what a witch his former wife was, are bound to taint their new relationships. Rather than remaining judgmental and belittling the ex-mate, it is more productive to ask, "Now that I am single, what have I learned from my past relationship about myself and what can I do now to make my life more satisfying?"

3. Self-pity. Next to blame, which can be turned inward in the form of depression or outward in the form of anger, self-pity is the most damaging emotional reaction. Too many unhappy divorces are embroiled in self-pity to live in the present or plan for the future. They repeat and reinforce former destructive patterns, see themselves as helpless victims, suffer from a succession of ailments and fatigue. The more energy and time they put into self-pity, the less they have available for building a new life.

4. Unrealistic expectations. Some people have very unrealistic expectations of how other people should be. They demand a perfect world with perfect human beings and become angry, frustrated, or withdrawn when things don't go their way. Since reality hardly ever measures up to their superstandards, they have a good excuse for not attempting any new undertaking or socializing. Since they anticipate a negative, disappointing consequence before they start, a start is never initiated. The failure here is to accept that we live in an imperfect world and that all the people in it are also imperfect. Disappointments are necessary for growth, change, and development. If a person is not willing to accept the fallibility of other human beings and life's inevitable frustrations, the chances for fulfillment are small indeed.

5. Fatalism. The fifth and final barrier is the mythical belief that most human unhappiness is caused by other people and outside events and that we have virtually no control over our own destiny. Blaming, stereotypic thinking, self-pity, and other similar behaviors are all symptomatic of this self-avoidant view; these are ways we avoid responsibility for our own self-created misery.

In contrast to the "I am a victim of my circumstances" philosophy is one that expresses self-responsibility: "I have the capacity to change and find greater fulfillment." In most areas of human interaction, there are few things that cannot be accomplished. If you think "I can't face my employer and request a raise; I can't live a healthier lifestyle; I can't get back into the social scene," ask yourself the following questions: If someone pointed a gun at your head and threatened to kill you if you didn't do what you say you can't do, would you do it? If your child or some other person very dear to you was in a life-threatening danger and their only salvation lay in your doing what you say you can't do, would you do it? If the answer to either of these questions is yes, then ask yourself, "How is it that I won't do things for my own happiness?"

These, then, are some of the factors that impede successful living during and after a divorce: stereotypic thinking, blaming, self-pity, unrealistic expectations, and fatalism. Support and sustained help from friends who not only offer a shoulder to cry on but also the reassurance that they wholly accept and value you can help the reconstructive process. Time is also important—wounds close slowly. Meaningful activities, social service, politics, college classes, and various self-improvement regimens also prove helpful for many people. Most critical is a hard and painful effort directed toward altering self-defeating attitudes. For this, professional assistance or a local self-help divorce group may be beneficial.

How do you know when the wounds of the separation and divorce process are healing properly? Mel Krantzler (1973) in his sensitive book, *Creative Divorce*, offers some guidelines, summarized here:

> Resentment toward your former mate has diminished in intensity, duration and frequency. You become more concerned with solving problems than complaining about them. You re-establish contact with old friends and begin making new friends, convinced that having divorced does not shame you. You begin making decisions and living a single life doing things based on your interests and pleasure—taking a course, attending a play, entertaining friends.

Sound Thinking and Smart Moves

1. Your feelings of betrayal and loss typically subside over time. If you create a new life there is a day when you will be pleased that you were able to break free from a painful relationship and live a life without hurt and despair.

2. Do not speak poorly of your partner to your kids. Kids do not need to know about adult topics in terms of infidelity. This person is still their other parent whom they love.

3. One person's choice to be unfaithful is not the other's fault. But, as you move forward and consider other relationships, think about what you can learn from the one that failed.

Chapter 9

SEEKING PROFESSIONAL HELP

MAKING THE DECISION

Howard Gardner, the influential Harvard theorist states in his book, *Frames of Mind* (2011), "My intelligence does not stop at my skin." To paraphrase Dr. Gardner's intention, it is an indication of wisdom to access resources when they are necessary and are likely to increase the likelihood of success.

After an affair, couples who want to rebuild their relationship are likely to have at least some ambivalence about staying in the relationship versus working toward separating in a constructive way. One partner may want to reconcile, while the other is still ambivalent or has decided to leave. Either way, painful and strong emotions will get activated inside and outside of the therapy room. The injured partner feels angry and very hurt, while the involved partner commonly struggles with feelings of shame and guilt.

A case in point: Barbara and Mark. They have been married for twelve years and have two sons. During the last year, Barbara, the VP of a software company, had been involved with another man with whom she did business. She didn't know whether to leave her husband or to break up the affair and try to work on improving their marriage. She decided to work on her marriage and suggested to Mark that they go for couples therapy. Mark was bitter and complained that therapy would be a waste of money: "I'm not crazy. You'd better straighten yourself out or leave. I'm staying in this house; I'm not leaving my children just because you've had a change of heart. I raised them!"

Barbara wasn't about to give up her home or children. She continued her plea for a third party until Mark reluctantly agreed to give therapy a try. Barbara and Mark give a summary account of their experience; Mark comments first:

"At the time Barbara suggested therapy, I was enraged. I'm a decent guy. I try to do the right thing. I've been home caring for the kids! This is what I get in return? I thought, 'Goddamn it, I don't deserve this!' Besides being angry as hell, I was embarrassed. Going to a stranger and telling him that when I roll over toward my wife in bed I feel her tense up isn't my ideal way to spend an evening!"

Barbara had this to say:

"I broke a cardinal rule by getting involved with a business colleague. It was the collision of opportunity and temptation. I knew I was driving Mark up the wall. He was starting to drink too much and he wasn't sleeping well at all. He was doing everything to contain himself. I really didn't see why I wasn't happy in my marriage. Why couldn't I get as much from Mark as I got from this other guy? Did I view Mark differently because he took on the house-husband role? I knew the only way I was going to work this out was with a couples therapist.

"One of the early things the therapist said to us was, 'I'm not going to make decisions for you; but I am going to help you clarify your issues and give you direction for healing the relationship. It will be up to you to follow through.' I felt a little taken back by his statement. I guess I was expecting to be told what to do."

Mark: In therapy, I was encouraged to be more expressive and this felt good. I began to say a lot of things to Barbara that I hadn't said before. But things between us got worse. I said to the therapist, "You suggested I communicate more, really express what I'm feeling, and when I do express what I'm feeling, what do I get back? Shit!" I was getting just what I got as a child. When I opened my mouth, I got a slap. We were encouraged not to give up; we were reminded that pain is not a signal to run.

Barbara: After five months of therapy, we began to see some real changes in our relationship. The biggest thing that happened was we began to appreciate each other as individuals—adult individuals. I viewed Mark more as the man he is, rather than something less than the power-brokers I deal with every day. I learned that he had been so preoccupied with taking care of me and the kids that he was suffocating. We did some reshuffling and it was a tremendous relief for him not to have all the responsibility of running the house. This was actually liberating for both of us. In therapy, we both began to appreciate—if not always liking—each other's honest thoughts and feelings. We didn't feel we had to be overly careful about hurting each other or causing one of us to fall apart. We began to believe in each other's strength. I regret it took me so long to realize how much his support meant to me.

Mark: Finally after several more months, we made a joint decision to terminate therapy. We wanted to do things on our own. It's not that all our problems went away. There wasn't anything magical like that. We just began to feel more like struggling with them without any extra help. I guess we had come to a point where we felt we understood and appreciated each other. I was feeling a sense of forgiveness, rather than a cloud of resentment and anger as well as hurt. We felt we could live our lives and be fulfilled even without each other. Also, for the first time in years, we were genuinely cooperative and positive with each other. We learned to compromise to our mutual benefit. Our relationship took a mature turn. We became more desirous of each other and truly enjoyed each other's company.

In this successful marital therapy experience, Mark and Barbara were helped in several ways, some of which may not be evident from their brief description. They were assisted to:

- Understand the underlying dynamic from their family-of-origin impacting their relationship;
- Develop clear communication so that the message sent is the message received;
- Identify the behavioral patterns and attitudes that were deteriorating their relationship;
- Take responsibility for their part of the relationship disruption rather than blame the other;
- Practice tactics designed to increase cooperative, relationship-promoting patterns and decrease negative, relationship-eroding patterns;
- Develop the ability to negotiate and create workable compromises rather than engaging in demoralizing fights;
- Work toward an atmosphere of forgivingness.

These are critical areas of intervention. To the extent that a breakdown occurs in one or more of these areas, relationship distress is likely to increase. A couple seeking assistance from a competent therapist can expect help in each of these areas.

Barbara and Mark got lucky. Without thorough checking, they ended up getting competent assistance. Don't depend on luck, not all credentialed therapists are the same.

Here are some preliminary screening suggestions:

- It is important in a prior telephone call or initial session to obtain information regarding the therapist's credentials and point of view. Postgraduate training (Fellowship, clinical diploma, etc.) is a plus.
- Beware of the therapist who imposes personal biases (e.g., insists on a particular lifestyle). This does not mean that therapists are not to have personal beliefs or that they are not to be expressed, only that they be honestly labeled as biases and not imposed.
- Therapists who view their role consistently as a judicial one in which they sift the evidence presented and eventually make pronouncements are, at best, inexperienced.

This approach tends to be extremely damaging because the partners involved are likely to devote their energy and ingenuity to digging up "evidence" against each other. The result is an escalation of bad feelings and an increased schism until the therapy and the relationship break down altogether.

- Therapists who side with one or the other partner on an overall basis ("You're the problem") rather than as a temporary therapeutic maneuver or on a particular issue, are reinforcing the false idea that at the heart of couple problems is a victim or a villain.

- Accusing each other and blaming the relationship disturbance on each other is decidedly counterproductive. Bitter quarreling over pointless issues, particularly if it goes on session after session and is encouraged by the therapist, is an indication of an incompetent therapist for allowing the destructive behavior to continue.

DANGER SIGNALS

How does a couple know if therapy is warranted? As we've seen, when an affair is discovered it is wise to consider couples therapy since the experience of discovery is so emotionally unsettling. But there are also sound and wise decisions to see a therapist to shore up a relationship even if it is not complicated by an affair. Relationship distress may range from overt anger to underground dissatisfaction taking the form of avoidance. Aside from the discovery or suspicion of an affair, the most obvious "red flags" indicating that a couple should consider getting the assistance of a professional third party are these:

- Frequent arguments without resolution in which one or both partners are left with hurt feelings or burning resentment.

- Feelings of being mistrusted for real or imagined reasons, or being suspicious of your partner ("How does she *really* spend her days off, she's always so evasive when I try pinning her down").

- Frequent avoidance of each other. There are numerous ways people living together can avoid each other. Sometimes a couple manages to have other people around all the time—frequent house guests, friends for dinner, friends to share vacations, friends to spend weekends with—hardly ever giving themselves an opportunity to be alone. These are usually the couples whose divorce shocks their friends who thought they were "wonderfully happy together." Television is another convenient barrier. Overwork or over-involvement in non-couple recreational pursuits can also be a danger signal. And, of course, paying more attention to one's phone, e-mail, and texts than to each other is not a good sign.

- Over-dependence on the part of one or both partners. This can be expressed by constant "checking" on each other, not feeling comfortable and worthwhile without a mate's companionship, resentment of a mate's independent interests, living for a spouse's achievements, and being overly sensitive to a spouse's criticism.

- Sexual dissatisfaction. This includes lack of attraction, inability to "let go" in bed, a lack of affection, warmth, and mutual sexual pleasuring.

These are some of the more common danger signals; there are an infinite number of variations. When should you seek help?

Not after a short-lived, shallow dip in domestic satisfaction. A day's arguing over the children, a few days of melancholy or self-pity, a siege of jealousy, these are not necessarily signals of trouble. They are more probably results of the normal strain of living. The key to watch for is repetition, a pattern consisting of resentment, boredom, loneliness, hurt, and sexual dissatisfaction.

WHAT *NOT* TO EXPECT FROM THERAPY

When we are little children and we fall, bruising our knee, Mommy or Daddy kisses the injury and makes it all better. They do magic. When we go to the doctor and he or she gives us a prescription that cures our ailment, the doctor does magic. When we are grown-up and have relationship problems, we go to another type of doctor, the relationship doctor, expecting that he or she will make the relationship all better, like magic. Unfortunately, therapy doesn't work that way. There are no magic pills, no magic wands to wave.

A passive stance—"therapy will make us all better"—is an unrealistic passive attitude that guarantees therapeutic failure. This is probably the most common unrealistic expectation that couples bring to therapy, and it is probably similar to the erroneous attitude that the primary relationship will prosper by itself: "Now that we're committed, the relationship will grow." Most of us are aware of the falsity of the latter notion, but it is a tempting trap. Relationships work because we work at it. This applies equally to therapy.

Additional expectations that increase the likelihood of dissatisfaction with therapy are these:

- Couples therapy is a process designed to keep the relationship together. This is not true. Therapy is supposed to help couples clarify their own needs, wishes, and feelings and to identify in their partner those patterns that meet their needs and those that do not. The attitude of a professional is likely to be: My job is to help these people stay together more compatibly and productively or to help them separate as amiably as possible if that is what they choose—the choice is theirs, not mine.

- "The couples therapist, being an intelligent individual, will see my side of things and straighten out my spouse who is really the problem." Very often this is the hidden agenda. However, if the therapist takes sides, the therapy may seem to be going well for the "righteous mate" but the relationship is likely to deteriorate. A more productive attitude involves the understanding that relationships are systemic, partners form a system, and like any system one part impacts the other.

- "I should feel comfortable throughout therapy." It is not comfortable to change behavioral patterns and couple dynamics. Consequently, the therapeutic process is likely to be painful at times. Serenity is hard to maintain, while sensitive issues are being brought to awareness and confronted as never before. Also, the progress of the partners is likely to be uneven so that when one opens up, the other may rebuff him or her. Result: hurt and angry feelings. Sensitive therapists will support the rebuffed partner, encouraging that partner not to give up while helping the other to be more responsive. But it still hurts. Discomfort in therapy is unavoidable; and a total absence of any discomfort is a sign that the process is merely superficial.

- "If we are sincere and work hard, things will improve immediately." Change is not easy and it is not instant. A relationship may even worsen before it gets better. Dissatisfaction, hurt feelings, anger, and misunderstanding are not quickly cleared up. Yet people tend, after a few sessions, to conclude things are all better. Frequently, this is a premature decision based on an avoidance of further exploration of "hot" issues.

- "We can always go into therapy in the future; things aren't that bad now." One of the biggest frustrations of couples therapists is that couples hesitate to seek help until the situation is desperate. Then they come to the therapist and expect to be bailed out. By this time, the relationship may have been severely damaged and the willingness to work at it almost exhausted. It is very difficult to help relationships that are extremely disturbed. They often break up in the end, and the partners unfairly ridicule the skills of the therapist when, in fact, a Solomon couldn't have prevented the breakup. If these same couples had begun therapy earlier, before things became intolerable, they could have been spared years of suffering and misery.

TYPES OF COUPLES THERAPISTS

Successful therapy relationships depend less on the professional's title than on training, experience, and personal qualities. Yet, knowing something about the classes of therapists makes for a more informed choice. The three major classes of mental health practitioners are psychiatrists, psychologists, and social workers. Professionally trained marriage counselors, mental health counselors, and nurse practitioners also offer treatment services to the public. A brief discussion of several of the major practitioners follows.

PSYCHIATRISTS

Psychiatrists are physicians who have completed medical training and have obtained a medical degree (MD or DO). Rather than extensive formal and extensive training in the psychology of relationship problems or supervised experience in helping persons solve their most pressing problems, many psychiatrists are primarily schooled in handling patients administratively with drugs and hospitalization—and giving psychological first aid. Consequently, many psychiatrists, particularly those trained in recent years, specialize in diagnosing and providing psycho-pharmacological treatment rather than psychotherapy.

Psychiatrists who have completed the requirements of the American Board of Psychiatry have usually spent approximately three or four years in psychiatric residence beyond the four years in medical school and a general (medical) internship. A part of the residency is usually at a large psychiatric institution such as a city or state hospital. In this setting, the people treated by the psychiatrist are likely to be severely disturbed, such as schizophrenics or chronic alcoholics.

Some of the training period, usually about six months, is spent working with neurological problems (disorders caused by pathological abnormalities of the brain or nerves) and some time is frequently devoted to work in an outpatient clinic, where the physician sees a variety of patients with a variety of problems.

Some psychiatrists doing psychotherapy and couples therapy rely heavily on medical methods, especially the administration of psychoactive drugs. This is most common among those with insufficient advanced training in individual and couples therapy. Such a psychiatrist is likely to prescribe drugs in an effort to "give the patient something." Unfortunately, problems of living are rarely solved by drugs.

How can you ascertain psychiatrists' methods of practice? Asking someone who has seen him or her in therapy may be helpful. A psychiatrist may briefly discuss his or her orientation in a telephone conversation.

If nothing is known except that a psychiatrist is qualified (with an MD and certification from the American Board of Psychiatry), an initial consultation is wise. The couple should arrange to meet the therapist together and jointly ask about methods and point of view.

Asking pointed questions of the therapist as to training, experience, and attitudes may seem rude or unnecessary, but remember that therapy is an important and expensive venture whose success depends, in part, upon the choice of the proper therapist. Couples may have to visit two or three different psychiatrists before finding an individual with whom they both feel comfortable, confident and who has sufficient training in couples therapy.

PSYCHOLOGISTS

A professional psychologist is an individual who has a doctoral degree from an accredited university or professional school in a program that is approved by the American Psychological Association. The doctoral degree takes five years beyond the four-year college degree to complete. This includes a one-year supervised full-time internship. All states have laws regulating the practice of psychologists. In the case of psychological practice that involves service for a fee (such as couples therapy), appropriate registration, certification, or licensing is required. All states forbid anyone not so registered, certified, or licensed to represent to the public that they are a psychologist and are eligible to treat patients with personal and couple issues with psychotherapy.

Since a psychologist does not have a medical degree (in psychology the doctorate is the PhD, EdD, or PsyD), he or she is not permitted to prescribe drugs in most states. If pharmaceutical therapy is deemed necessary, the psychologist will refer the patient to a psychiatrist for consultation and a prescription.

All psychologists are concerned with the dynamics of personality and behavior but their training varies considerably. As a group, psychologists have far more extensive training in principles of human behavior than the general run of psychiatrist or social worker, but not all may have had specialized training in applying their knowledge to couple issues. Some have a strong background in other areas, for example, treating substance abuse or anxiety disorders that have only modest relevance to couples therapy.

Psychologists in the private (or agency) practice of individual and couples therapy usually have a background in the more therapy-relevant specialties of clinical or counseling psychology, but it is wise to ask the practitioner about his or her specific experience. Psychologists who are board certified by the American Board of Professional Psychologists (ABPP) have passed a three-part postdoctoral exam demonstrating advanced competence.

SOCIAL WORKERS

The minimum standard for a professional social worker is a master's degree in social work (MSW) earned by the completion of a rigorous two-year program of graduate study in an accredited school of social work. In addition to receiving the required classroom instruction, candidates for the degree work two or three days a week in an agency that offers counseling services, such as a psychiatric clinic, a hospital, a probation department, a welfare department, or a family counseling clinic.

This internship, spread over two years, is supervised by an experienced social worker who holds the MSW degree. Usually, individuals accepted into a graduate school of social work have an undergraduate degree (BS or BA) in one of the social or behavioral sciences.

Most states have laws which license or certify the practice of social work and there is national certification by the Academy of Social Work as well as strong local, state, and national (National Academy of Social Work) organizations that strive to enforce professional standards. Most social agencies are sensitive to professional standards and in only a few, such as departments of county welfare, is the term "social worker" used for individuals who do not have the MSW degree.

A couple desiring therapy would normally not be applying for this service at a welfare agency but at a family counseling service where the professional degree is required for employment. In seeking a private practitioner, an inquiry as to whether the individual has earned the master's degree in social work from an accredited institution is warranted.

It is important to ask all practitioners, including social workers questions regarding his or her professional experience. One pertinent question may be,

"Have you had supervised experience in couples therapy?" Typically, social work students are offered a general program during their two years of training. This includes group work, individual casework, and community organization. A few social work schools provide for specialization in one of these areas. Thus, a student interested in training in couples and family therapy may be assigned a family counseling agency for internship. Others may obtain specialized training after obtaining the graduate degree.

Although social workers are frequently given less status by the public and by other professionals, with appropriate training, they are as qualified to do couples therapy as psychiatrists and psychologists trained in this area.

MARRIAGE AND FAMILY THERAPISTS

To belong to the American Association of Marriage and Family Therapy, the practitioner must have a master's degree in marriage and family therapy or a closely related field, and two years postgraduate supervised clinical training. Those individuals with a degree in marital and family therapy are licensed in all states and their title is "Marriage Counselor." Their training in the specific area of marital and family therapy is extensive.

In addition to the aforementioned practitioners, nurse practitioners have a master's degree or its equivalent in nursing with a specialization in psychiatric nursing and may also do couples therapy. Since their background is not exclusive to psychotherapy, it is wise to choose someone who has additional training in couples therapy. Professional counselors and pastoral counselors are also licensed in most states and must have a minimum of a master's degree and postgraduate, supervised experience, same applies—best to inquire about specific training in couples therapy.

THE SEARCH

Finding a satisfactory therapist is often difficult. Sometimes recommendations made by friends, physicians, and lawyers are useful; other times they are not—a therapist who is quite helpful to one couple may not be helpful at all to another. Public reputation is often a clue, but sometimes the popular therapist is the one who pleases rather than effectively intervenes.

Some couples therapists without strong credentials are very talented. However, in a field where incompetence and fraud are not uncommon, it is safer to choose a therapist who has had reputable training and experience. Unfortunately, professional qualifications do not indicate whether a therapist has had minimal, uninspired, or top-quality preparation—questioning on background is warranted. Further, since all forms of therapy are a mixture of art and science, the personality of the therapist is also important.

A couples therapist may be a happily coupled man or woman who accepts life, committed relationships, and people, or a dour individual whose own relationship is sterile and who approaches relationship problems with a "what can you expect" attitude.

Sometimes couples therapists are very directive in their approach, to the point of becoming impatient or irritated if their clients fail to follow their suggestions immediately; sometimes they are so timidly nondirective that their clients feel they are providing the therapist with an interesting hour of conversation and gaining nothing in return. Occasionally, a practitioner will have a moralistic attitude toward sex, divorce, or life itself that is conveyed in judgmental proclamations about "right and wrong." Or, the therapist may have an irresponsible, "liberated," egotistical attitude that causes confusion and uncertainty.

Even the best therapist with the best training is bound to have bad days and is certain to do better with some couples than with others. However well intentioned, a therapist's interventions may not always be effective. The mark of a professional is not perfection; it is a willingness to admit mistakes and learn from them.

It should be clear by now that you must do some homework in choosing a couples therapist. Obviously, these warnings can be used to provide justification for those who wish to avoid therapy or who want to quit because the going is rough. This is not the spirit in which the cautions have been offered.

Competent professional intervention has improved many ailing relationships; effective therapists have helped couples to reconsider their relationship and move in more constructive directions; this type of exploration is not being discouraged. The point is that to increase your chances of reaping the very real benefits of therapy, you should be able to evaluate a therapist with some sophistication.

In making a decision about a therapist, your own judgment is critical. A poor choice is bad enough when you're buying something that has only limited impact on our life. But you are depending on a couples therapist to help you repair serious issues. A poor choice can have far-reaching consequences. With an incompetent therapist, a problem that may have been repairable can worsen to the point of no return.

ASSESSING THE THERAPIST

Given the importance of the decision, after credentials, personal qualities, and reputation have been considered, the final decision as to compatibility rests on the couple's shoulders. The most effective way of deciding is to get referrals from several sources, including professional associations, friends, and other professionals, and to shop around, especially if there is ambivalence with previous consultations.

Admittedly, this procedure can be expensive because a few visits to a therapist may be necessary before a reasonable judgment can be made; it is also possible that the first therapist chosen will prove to be quite suitable. To aid in making a realistic appraisal of the therapist, a list of seventeen questions, follows.

Responses are scored from 0 to 4; 0 equals never or not at all; 1 slightly or occasionally; 2 sometimes or moderately; 3 a great deal or most of the time; and 4 markedly or all of the time.

Use a pencil to write in the number that best reflects your feelings and observations and then obtain a total score.

1. The therapist appears interested in working with us.
2. The therapist uses words and language that make sense to us, not "psychobabble."
3. The therapist listens carefully to what we say and asks relevant questions that demonstrate that he/she is paying attention.
4. In the presence of the therapist, it is not implied that we are "odd, weird or in any way that is defamatory."
5. The therapist is open to different points of view. He or she is not fixed on "one right way" to handle an issue.
6. The therapist gives us the opportunity to work out solutions with help, rather than simply telling us what to do.
7. The therapist confronts us with his or her concerns when it is beneficial to our relationship.
8. The therapist does not resist being direct when situations require immediate action.
9. We believe that the therapist has our best interests at heart.
10. The therapist behaves in a manner that assumes we are equals, rather than placing him- or herself on a pedestal.
11. The therapist spontaneously volunteers aspects of his or her life when it is useful.
12. When we ask directly, the therapist is receptive to discussing his or her personal life to the extent that it is beneficial to us.
13. The therapist is open to seeing other people in our life when necessary, or to giving us sound reasons for not inviting others into the treatment setting.
14. The therapist admits, nondefensively, when he or she doesn't know something.
15. The therapist is open to listening nondefensiveness when we differ.
16. Overall, even when we leave feeling sad, it's not because we feel the therapist has given up on us.
17. We feel that we are learning a lot about our relationship and our part in it.

A perfect score on this instrument (68) is most unlikely. A rating above the mid-forties is an indication of a sound choice; a rating between thirty-five and forty is borderline. A score below that is indicative of a poor choice.

In couples therapy, it is important that the therapist chosen be acceptable to both partners because a big difference in is likely to add to an already strain-burdened relationship. As mentioned earlier, it may take several sessions before a reasonable judgment can be made. Sometimes there is an obvious match and a much quicker decision will be rendered.

COST AND LENGTH OF THERAPY

One of the most important considerations for many couples is the cost of therapy. The range is very broad and is complicated by the number of managed care companies that set fees for therapists on their panel. If it is affordable, it may be advantageous to see a therapist who is not part of managed care, the advantage being increased confidentiality and continuity of care without the dictates of an anonymous case manager who would like nothing better than to have treatment terminated.

Community agencies and family institutes, both public and private, generally have lower fee schedules and may even have a sliding scale based on income. Listings of these agencies are available on the Internet. Here are several suggestions regarding fees:

It is wise not to become involved with a therapist whose fees you will not be able to afford on a weekly basis for at least several months.

When there is legitimate financial reason, it is not "impolite" to ask if a therapist will reduce the fee in the initial phone call. Some will, others won't. Most won't offer unless asked.

Do not regard size of fee as a reflection of ability. There is no relationship. Some competent therapists have a relatively low fee schedule; others bordering on incompetence are exorbitant.

Whatever the fee, it is not unusual to feel resentful. Payment for an intangible service is hard to accept. Most payments result in something that can be driven, eaten, worn, or shown off. Therapy provides none of these.

Just as fee schedules vary, so do recommendations concerning the frequency with which a couple need to see the therapist and the length of time the therapy takes. In many instances, it will be suggested that therapy occur once a week jointly for forty-five to sixty minutes. Sometimes treatment is warranted more often, and sometimes less.

If the relationship difficulties are quite serious, therapy is likely to continue for one or two years, or even longer. It may be on a weekly basis, especially initially it may be more frequent, but as progress is made, the frequency will be decreased. Sometimes, although the problems appear severe at first glance, progress is established in a relatively short time and methods for continuing progress without therapy is suggested. Conversely, some issues that appear minor may not be so minor and take longer than assumed to resolve. A discovered infidelity obviously is not minor, and treatment is likely to be intense and be longer term.

Regardless of the duration of therapy, it is doubtful that progress will proceed in a neat forward direction. Rather, periods of stagnation, or even backsliding, are to be expected. Freud termed these reverses "negative therapeutic reactions" and ascribed them to an unconscious sense of guilt that barred improvement. While there is good reason to believe that Freud's explanation is ill-suited to the dynamics of many people, periods of "two steps back" and stagnation is part of even the most successful therapy experiences.

WHAT ARE THE ODDS FOR SUCCESS?

If we follow the research in this area, the trail is very narrow. There is a paucity of research on the effectiveness of couple therapy when there has been an infidelity. In fact, the literature on outcomes of couple therapy for infidelity is based on twenty-five infidelity couples in the United States and 145 infidelity couples in Germany and Austria. However, there is no shortage on the deleterious impact that infidelity has on a primary relationship (Allen & Rhoades, 2008; Atkins et al., 2005; Cano & O'Leary, 2000).

Despite the devastating effects infidelity has on a primary relationship, the treatment studies that have been completed suggest that couples can be successfully treated (Atkins et al., 2005; Atkins et al., 2010; Gordon et al., 2004). Couples in whom there has been an affair who pursue marital therapy have shown strong improvements during therapy, including greater marital satisfaction, reduced psychological trauma symptoms, and greater forgiveness in the uninvolved partner.

While those results are encouraging, it has remained unclear whether the gains obtained in treatment were sustained past the six-month follow-up (Atkins et al., 2010; Gordon et al., 2004). However, a recent study (Marín et al., 2014) takes the focus further. The post-therapy outcomes of nineteen infidelity couples were assessed approximately every six months for five years post-therapy. In addition to the couples where there had been infidelity reported, there were also couples with "secret" infidelity that was discovered or revealed after treatment and couples where there had not been infidelity.

Although the sample of "current infidelity revealed" and "undisclosed (secret) infidelity" couples are small, the data suggest differences in marital outcomes between these two types of affairs. Among the revealed infidelity couples, more than half (57%) the couples remained married by the five-year follow-up, whereas only 20 percent of the secret infidelity couples were still married by the five-year follow-up, compared with 77 percent of non-infidelity couples. Although these differences need to be viewed within the small sample of infidelity couples generally, the current results suggest that more than half of the revealed infidelity couples were able to sustain the gains made during treatment and preserve the integrity of the relationship.

Sound Thinking and Smart Moves

1. What happens in the consulting room is important, but even more important is what happens outside the consulting room. Experienced therapists suggest occasional experiences to consider between meetings (e.g., "please discuss . . . practice this. . ."); following through on these outside-the-office experiences are critical to a positive outcome of treatment.

2. During therapy sessions phones should be shut off and out of sight. Focus should be exclusive to the treatment, leaving other issues for other times. Of course this applies to the therapist as well. Picking up the phone during a session is rude. If there is a pending emergency that may be an exception, but it should be noted to the couple and their time restored.

3. Speak up to the therapist if something bothers you about therapy. Openness and respectfully discussing disagreement is crucial. Avoiding discussion when something said (or not said, that you feel is an omission) is akin to withdrawing and is similar to what happens in primary relationships. Bear in mind that withdrawal is a well-researched factor that leads to alienation—in all kinds of relationships.

EPILOGUE

When I wrote about extra-relationship affairs years ago, I didn't have a lot of experience treating couples who were struggling with an affair. The written work was more journalistic than clinical, but it made quite a splash in the media as sex frequently does, especially if it touches a nerve, as infidelity is bound to do. I didn't have enough experience at the time to realize that infidelity is perhaps the most complex issue encountered by couple therapists. The work with couples when it is straightforward, without complication is hard enough, but when infidelity is added to the mix it often challenges even seasoned couples therapists. Some examples that have come up and make the work even more complex:

1. A couple has seen a therapist for a few visits, always conjoint. At the first visit, the therapist explained that the alliance was to the couple. Consequently, he asserted, don't call or text and begin by saying, "Don't tell my partner, but. . ."

   Despite that admonition, one partner showed up alone for a session, contending her mate was called out of town last minute for a business crisis. She then tells the therapist she is having an affair.

HOW DOES THE THERAPIST PROTECT THE WIFE'S DISCLOSURE WHILE BEING FAIR TO THE HUSBAND?

2. A therapist is seeing a couple. The wife has become aware that her husband has a mistress. At one point, his wife turns to him and states she is going to the police about some illegal behavior on his part. Her husband responds with a counter threat.

WHAT IS THE THERAPIST TO DO?

3. A couple presents with an affair by the husband. He strongly contends that the affair is over and he has no contact with his former paramour. However, one night the therapist spots the husband at a local bar with a woman who is not his wife; by his contact with the woman she appears to be more than a friend, much more. The husband didn't see the therapist.

WHAT'S THE THERAPIST'S NEXT MOVE?

4. A married patient discloses boundary violations she initiated with a therapist she and her husband had seen previously and still see periodically. The current therapist is acquainted with the therapist in question. The patient would like to bring in her husband and begin conjoint therapy. She is vague as to the current out-of-bounds relationship with the former therapist.

GIVEN THE POSSIBILITY OF AN ONGOING INAPPROPRIATE RELATIONSHIP WITH THE FORMER THERAPIST, WHAT ARE THE IMPLICATIONS FOR THE CURRENT TREATMENT, AND WHAT IS THE CURRENT THERAPIST'S ETHICAL RESPONSIBILITY?

5. A female patient whose initial complaint was relationship issues confides after three visits that the lover she has been discussing is married. She wants to bring in her lover, stating that he really wants to leave his wife but they need to work out some of their differences.

HOW DOES THE THERAPIST RESPOND TO THE PATIENT AND TO HER REQUEST?

And the complications continue. . .

Keeping the potential complications in mind, as well as basic treatment considerations, I recall having a serious case of the jitters on my first national TV program, one of the morning news shows. A split second before we went on the air, I noticed the interviewer's fly was open. Oddly, that calmed me down. Maybe I wasn't the only one with the jitters. The first question asked of me was whether I had affairs. I glanced slyly at the open fly as I answered in the negative. A decade or so, and several marriages later for the interviewer, I read a piece about the interviewer that justified my sly smile. It appears the interviewer had a well-earned reputation as a "play around" kind of person with several failed marriages.

After my interview I passed Charles Evers, the brother of the late civil rights champion Medgar Evers, in the hallway, and he whispered to me, "Your numbers are way too low." He was referring to my estimate of the percentage of men and women in committed relationships who had affairs. He was probably right then, and would still probably be right today since most people are apprehensive to admit to having been unfaithful; consequently, even as they are updated from time to time, the published figures are likely to always be an underestimate.

Now, so many years later as a psychologist specializing in treating couples and sexual issues, I have accumulated a few decades more experience. What have I learned that stands out? I've learned that it is wise to be prepared for the treatment traps clinicians treating affair-involved couples are likely to encounter. Further, most clinicians, including myself, don't have all the answers; couples work is not for the beginner. Further, when there is an affair, it requires experience with this issue as well as colleagues to confer with from time to time as needed, in addition to keeping up with the relevant research that applies to practice.

The alliance in couple therapy is to both partners, but what if one partner calls, or shows up alone and confides an affair-involvement? The clinician is in a difficult position. During the next conjoint session when the other partner asks of his or her affair-involved partner, "Why is it that I was unable to reach you last Wednesday evening?" the clinician knows and the affair-involved knows. The noninvolved partner is looking for an answer that all the others in the room have but are not eager to share.

What to do? As noted, some couple therapists state at the outset, "I don't want to hold secrets, so don't tell them to me." The drawback, of course, is that there may be a major factor that is undermining the relationship, and the therapist won't be privy to it because the involved member of the couple is reluctant to bring it to the fore.

But even with that admonition what if one partner shares a secret affair? What I've learned is to once again make clear to the affair-involved partner that my allegiance is not to him or her alone; it is couples therapy, not individual. Consequently, the couple bond has been broken and we cannot continue unless the affair-involved partner chooses to address the issue with his or her partner. If not, how to tell the noninvolved partner that we are not continuing? Actually, it's not my problem; it is up to the affair-involved partner to explain the abrupt termination of treatment—he or she has been warned. I've learned not to take responsibility that is not mine and that has not been easy for me, but there are times that being too helpful is not helpful.

I've learned that some views of affairs are unconventional but may have credibility, at least to some. I recall sitting in a clinical meeting with about a dozen clinicians from psychiatry, social work, and psychology. A psychologist was presenting a couples case and stated that the affair-involved husband contended, when caught, that his affair actually saved the marriage. What? It sounded like he was claiming that an affair was a sacrifice he was making for his family. My first thought was, "No, he didn't say that!" However, after I got over the shock and listened carefully I could see the point. He loved his wife, he had two children, one with special needs, but the marital relationship left him more than a little empty. Couples therapy didn't improve his satisfaction and divorce was not an option. His wife had a hard enough time coping even with his support; divorce, he believed, would break her. The affair, he claimed, was superficial—can getting naked with someone ever be superficial?—but it provided enough satisfaction to compensate for what he sorely missed in his marriage.

Sometimes a relationship needs three to survive. It is certainly unconventional, but far from rare. Some affairs have run parallel to long-term marriages. Then there are the genetic factors we discussed earlier. We are a product of nature and nurture, but psychologists like myself are steeped in the factors of nurture, to the neglect of nature. Some people, men and women, by nature are not particularly restrained by the monogamous code; he or she will probably be more likely to step out. They are, by nature, varietists. We vary in predispositions. Just as some of us naturally tend toward being heavier despite having tried numerous diets, while others have less restraint and stay slender. Is this a pass to those who violate their partner's trust?

This is not to offer an excuse for the "wanderers," only to make the point that maintaining a monogamous relationship is more difficult for some, just as other factors are for others. If the marriage is not a close one, these affairs may be unnoticed and without major consequence. They may even have the positive effect of keeping a marriage that is satisfactory in most respects, alive and intact. If the marriage is a close one, a strain, like an undiagnosed virus is going to undermine love, and if discovered, a crisis is likely to develop even if the affair is casual.

Of course, few of those on the betrayal end of an affair will not find anything casual or of minor consequence if it is discovered—and "I'm genetically predisposed to variety" is not likely to go over well with the offended. That's understandable; the impact is anything but casual. More likely, it is often profound shock followed by hurt and anger. It has also occurred to me, after some experience, that discovery is often not purely accidental. When a man leaves his mistress's underwear in the trunk of his wife's car, stupidity is one possible reason, but it is more likely a hidden wish to be discovered, hostility is also likely.

And what about the man I saw several years back who went on a vacation with his mistress and dropped his wife a postcard, signing off, "Wish you were her." That was the rare instance where one "e" too few changed lives.

As with all things, the prognosis for repair is always more positive if the status was decent beforehand. If the relationship was a mess and then the affair is discovered, it may be beyond repair. However, if the couple is game and will follow a repair prescription faithfully, the effort can result in a stronger relationship than before the affair. That has been my experience many times. In all areas of life, strong, unwavering commitment toward a goal is a very big advantage in the chase for success.

What I haven't learned is how to help save a relationship when one partner continues to lie in the face of a broken trust. Or how to assist a man or woman who is intent to destroy their life and the lives of their children by continuing in an affair that is like a drug and is likely to end as badly as drug abuse does. Most affairs don't end in a new primary relationship, and those that do often teeter on the unstable trust that initiated their alignment.

What I do know about what I don't know is why these failures bother me so much. I lost my father at age four and subsequently, my mother married and divorced twice. It was in Brooklyn, New York, during the 1950s and 1960s when the "D" word was uncommon and support and understanding unknown. I've experienced the impact of a broken family and after all my years of working with couples, it still breaks my heart when it occurs unnecessarily.

REFERENCES

Agnew, A., Christopher, R., et al. (1998, April). Cognitive interdependence: Commitment and the mental representation of close relationships. *Journal of Personality and Social Psychology*, 74(4), 939–954.

Ali, L., & Miller, L. (2004, July 12). The new infidelity: From office affairs to Internet hookups, more wives are cheating too. *Newsweek*, 46.

Allen, E. S., & Rhoades, G. K. (2008). Not all affairs are created equal: Emotional involvement with an extra-dyadic partner. *Journal of Sex and Marital Therapy*, 43, 307–317.

Allen, E. S., Rhoades, G. K., et al. (2008). Premarital precursors of marital infidelity. *Family Process*, 47(2), 243–259.

Amato, P. R., & Hohmann-Marriott, B. (2007). A comparison of high- and low-distress marriages that end in divorce. *Journal of Marriage and Family*, 69, 621–638.

American Association for Marriage and Family Therapy. (2013). https://www.aamft.org/iMIS15/AAMFT/Content/consumerupdates/infidelity.aspx.

American Psychological Association. http://www.apa.org/topics/divorce.

Atkins, D. C., Baucom, D. H., & Jacobson, N. S. (2001). Understanding infidelity: Correlates in a national random sample. *Journal of Family Psychology*, 15, 735–749.

Atkins, D. C., Dimidjian, S., & Jacobson, N. S. (2001). Why do people have affairs? Recent research and future directions about attributions for extramarital affairs. In *Attribution, Communication Behavior, and Close Relationships*, edited by V. Manusov & J. H. Harvey, 305–319. Cambridge, UK: Cambridge University Press.

Atkins, D. C., Eldridge, K. A., Baucom, D. H., & Christensen, A. (2005). Infidelity and behavioral couple therapy: Optimism in the face of betrayal. *Journal of Consulting and Clinical Psychology*, 73, 144–150.

Atkins, D. C., Marín, R. A., Lo, T. T., Klann, N., & Hahlweg, K. (2010). Outcomes of couples with infidelity in a community-based sample of couple therapy. *Journal of Family Psychology*, 24(2), 212.

Bach, George R., & Wyden, Peter. (1969). *The Intimate Enemy: How to Fight Fair in Love and Marriage*. New York: Basic Books.

Bachand, L. L., & Caron, S. L. (2001). Ties that bind: A qualitative study of happy long-term marriages. *Contemporary Family Therapy*, 23, 105–121.

Battle, C. L., & Miller, I. W. (2005). Families and forgiveness. In *Handbook of Forgiveness*, edited by Everett L. Worthington. New York: Routledge.

Bell, Robert R., & Peltz, Dorothyann. (1974). Extramarital sex among women. *Medical Aspects of Human Sexuality*, 8, 10.

Block, J. (2001). *Broken Promises, Mended Hearts: Maintaining Trust in Love Relationships*. Chicago, IL: Contemporary Books.

Block, J., & Bartell, S. (2002). *Mommy or Daddy, Whose Side Am I On?* Avon, MA: Adams Media.

Blow, A.J., & Hartnett, K. (2005). Infidelity in committed relationships II: A substantive review. *Journal of Marital and Family Therapy*, 31, 217–233.

Broderick, Carlfred B. (1970). Should a husband or wife confess infidelity? *Medical Aspects of Sexuality*, 5, 8–15.

Brown, E.M. (2001). *Patterns of Infidelity and Their Treatment* (2nd edition). Philadelphia, PA: Brunner-Routledge.

Buss, D.M., & Shackelford, T.K. (1997a). From vigilance to violence: Mate retention tactics in married couples. *Journal of Personality and Social Psychology*, 72, 346–361.

Buss, D.M., & Shackelford, T.K. (1997b). Susceptibility to infidelity in the first year of marriage. *Journal of Research in Personality*, 31, 193–221.

Butler, M.H., Harper, J.M., & Seedall, R.B. (2009). Facilitated disclosure versus clinical accommodation of infidelity secrets: An early pivot point in couple therapy. *Journal of Marital and Family Therapy*, 35(1), 125–143.

Cano, A., & O'Leary, D. (2000). Infidelity and separations precipitate major depressive episodes and symptoms of nonspecific depression and anxiety. *Journal of Consulting and Clinical Psychology*, 68, 774–781.

Chamy, I.W., & Pamass, S. (1995). The impact of extramarital relationships on the continuation of marriages. *Journal of Sex and Marital Therapy*, 21, 100–115.

Cramer, R.E., Manning-Ryan, B., Johnson, L.M., & Barbo, E. (2000). Sex differences in subjective distress to violations of trust: Extending an evolutionary perspective. *Basic and Applied Social Psychology*, 22(2), 101–109.

De Paulo, B. (2015). *Marriage vs. Single Life: How Science and the Media Got It So Wrong*. Seattle, WA: Amazon Digital Services.

Donnelly, Denise. (1993). Sexually inactive marriages. *Journal of Sex Research*, 30, 171–179.

Drigotas, S.M., Safstrom, C.A., & Gentilia, T. (1999). An investment model prediction of dating infidelity. *Journal of Personality and Social Psychology*, 77, 509–524.

Druckerman, P. (2007). *Lust in Translation: Infidelity from Tokyo to Tennessee*. New York: Penguin Books.

Easterling, B., Knox, D., & Brackett, A. (2012). Secrets in romantic relationships: Does sexual orientation matter? *Journal of GLBT Family Studies*, 8(2), 196–208.

Ellis, A. (2003). *Sex without Guilt in the 21st Century*. Fort Lee, NJ: Barricade Books.

Fife, S.T., Weeks, G.R., & Gambescia, N. (2008a). The intersystems approach to treating infidelity. In *Infidelity: A Practitioner's Guide to Working with Couples in Crisis*, edited by P. Peluso, 71–97. Philadelphia, PA: Routledge.

Fife, S.T., Weeks, G.R., & Gambeseia, N. (2008b). Treating infidelity: An integrative approach. *The Family Journal: Counseling and Therapy for Couples and Families*, 16, 316–323.

Fincham, F. D., Hall, J., & Beach, S. R. H. (2006). Forgiveness in marriage: Current status and future directions. *Family Relations*, 55, 415–427.

Fish, J.N., Pavkov, T.W., Wetchler, J.L., & Bercik, J. (2012). Characteristics of those who participate in infidelity: The role of adult attachment and differentiation in extradyadic experiences. *The American Journal of Family Therapy*, 40(3), 214–229.

Ford, Clellan S., & Beach, Frank A. (1951). *Patterns of Sexual Behavior*. New York: Harper and Brothers.

Friedman, Richard A. (2015, May 22). Infidelity lurks in your genes. *New York Times*, Sunday Review, 1.

Gardner, H. (2011). *Frames of Mind*. New York: Basic Books.

Glass, S.P. (2002). *Not "Just Friends": Protect Your Relationship from Infidelity and Heal the Trauma of Betrayal*. New York: Free Press.

Glass, S.P., & Wright, T.L. (1985). Sex differences in type of extramarital involvement and marital satisfaction. *Sex Roles*, 12, 1101–1119.

Glass, S.P., & Wright, T.L. (1992). Justifications for extramarital relationships: The association between attitudes, behaviors, and gender. *The Journal of Sex Research*, 29, 361–387.

Gordon, K.C., & Baucom, D.H. (2003). Forgiveness and marriage: Preliminary support for a synthesized model of recovery from a marital betrayal. *American Journal of Family Therapy*, 31, 179–199.

Gordon, K.C., Baucom, D.H., & Snyder, D.K. (2004). An integrative intervention for promoting recovery from extramarital affairs. *Journal of Marital and Family Therapy*, 30, 213–246.

Gordon, K.C., Baucom, D.H., & Snyder, D.K. (2005). Treating couples recovering from infidelity: An integrative approach. *Journal of Clinical Psychology*, 61, 1393–1405.

Gottman, J. (1993). The roles of conflict engagement, escalation, and avoidance in marital interaction: A longitudinal view of five types of couples. *Journal of Consulting and Clinical Psychology*, 61(1), 6.

Gottman, J. (1994a). *Why Marriages Succeed or Fail*. New York: Simon and Schuster.

Gottman, J. (1994b). *What Predicts Divorce? The Relationship between Marital Process and Marital Outcomes*. Mahwah, NJ: Lawrence Erlbaum.

Gottman, J. (2011). *Raising an Emotionally Intelligent Child*. New York: Simon and Schuster.

Gottman, J.M., & Levenson, W. (1999). Rebound from marital conflict and divorce prediction. *Family Process*, 38, 287–292.

Greene, B.L., Lee, R.R., & Lustig, N. (1974). Conscious and unconscious factors in marital infidelity. *Medical Aspects of Human Sexuality*, 8, 87–105.

Hall, J.H., & Fincham, F.D. (2005). Self-forgiveness: The stepchild of forgiveness research. *Journal of Social and Clinical Psychology*, 24(5), 621–637.

Hansen, G.L. (1987). Extra-dyadic relations during courtship. *Journal of Sex Research*, 23, 382–390.

Hooyman, Nancy R., & Kramer, Betty J. (2008). *Living through Loss: Interventions across the Life Span*. New York: Columbia University Press.

Hunt, Morton. (1971). *The Affair*. New York: New American Library.

Hunt, Morton. (1974). *Sexual Behavior in the 70s*. Chicago, IL: Playboy Press.

Johnson, R.E. (1970). Extramarital sexual intercourse: A methodological note. *Journal of Marriage and the Family*, 32, 249–255.

Jong, Erica. (1973). *Fear of Flying*. New York: Holt, Rinehart and Winston.

Kinsey, A.C., Pomeroy, W.B., & Martin, C.E. (1948). *Sexual Behavior in the Human Male*. Philadelphia, PA: W. B. Saunders Co.

Kinsey, A.C., Pomeroy, W.B., Martin, C.E., & Gebhard, P.H. (1953). *Sexual Behavior in the Human Female*. Philadelphia, PA: W. B. Saunders Co.

Koch, Joanne, & Koch, Lew. (1976). *The Marriage Savers*. New York: Coward, McCann & Georghegan, Inc.

Krantzler, Mel. (1973). *Creative Divorce*. New York: M. Evans and Co.

Kreider, R.M., & Ellis, R. (2011). Number, timing, and duration of marriages and divorces: 2009. Current Population Reports, P70–125. Washington, DC: U.S. Census Bureau.

Liu, C. (2000). A theory of marital sexual life. *Journal of Marriage and the Family*, 62, 363–374.

Llewellyn, Charles E. (1970). Should a husband or wife confess infidelity? *Medical Aspects of Human Sexuality*, 5, 14–15.

Lusterman, D.D. (2005). Helping children and adults cope with parental infidelity. *Journal of Clinical Psychology*, 61(11), 1439–1451.

Lyubomirsky, S. (2012, December 1). New love: Short shelf life. *New York Times*, 1.

Marín, Rebeca A., Christensen, Andrew, & Atkins, David C. (2014). Infidelity and behavioral couple therapy: Relationship outcomes over 5 years following therapy. *Couple and Family Psychology: Research and Practice*, 3(1), 1–12.

Moors, A.C., & Schechinger, H. (2014). Understanding sexuality: Implications of Rubin for relationship research and clinical practice. *Journal of Sexual and Relationship Therapy*, 29(4), 476–482.

Myers, Lonny, & Leggitt, Hunter. (1970). A new view of adultery. *Sexual Behavior*, 2, 52–62.

National Opinion Research Center at the University of Chicago. (1994, October 13). *The University of Chicago Chronicle*, 14(4).

Negash, S., Cui, M., Fincham, F.D., & Pasley, K. (2014). Extradyadic involvement and relationship dissolution in hetero-sexual women university students. *Archives of Sexual Behavior*, 43, 531–539.

Nemeth, J.M., Bonomi, A.E., et al. (2012, August). Sexual infidelity as trigger for intimate partner violence. *Journal of Women's Health*, 21(9), 942–949.

Nogales, A. (2009). *Parents Who Cheat. How Children and Adults Are Affected When Their Parents Are Unfaithful*. Deerfield Beach, FL: Health Communication.

Notarius, C.I., & Markman, H.J. (1993). *We Can Work It Out: Making Sense of Marital Conflict*. New York: Putnam.

Oberle, C.D., Dooley, Andrea, A., & Nagurney, J. (2016). Predicting perceived infidelity from gender and interpersonal traits. *Sexual and Relationship Therapy*, 1, 89–101.

O'Leary, K.D. (2005). Commentary on intrapersonal, interpersonal, and contextual factors in extramarital involvement. *Clinical Psychology: Science and Practice*, 12, 131–133.

Olson, M.M., Russell, C.S., Higgins-Kessler, M., & Miller, R.B. (2002). Emotional processes following disclosure of an extramarital infidelity. *Journal of Marital and Family Therapy*, 28, 423–434.

Omarzu, J., Miller, A., Schultz, C., & Timmerman, A. (2012). Motivations and emotional consequences related to engaging in extramarital relationships *International Journal of Sexual Health*, 24(2), 154–162.

Peluso, P.R., & Spina, P. (2008). Understanding infidelity: Pitfalls and lessons for couples counselors. *The Family Journal*, 16(4), 324–327.

Pike, James A. (1967). *You and the New Morality*. New York: Harper and Row.

Pittman, F.S. (1989). *Private Lies: Infidelity and the Betrayal of Intimacy*. New York: Norton.

Platt, R.A., Nalbone, D.P., Casanova, G.M., & Wetchler, J.L. (2008). Parental conflict and infidelity as predictors of adult children's attachment style and infidelity. *The American Journal of Family Therapy*, 36(2), 149–161.

Prins, K.S., Buunk, B.P., & Van Yperen, N.W. (1993). Equity, normative disapproval, and extramarital relationships. *Journal of Social and Personal Relationships*, 10, 39–53.

Reibstein, J., & Burbach, F. (2013). An increasingly convincing case for couples therapy. *Journal of Family Therapy*, 35, 225–228.

Rimmer, Robert. (1966). *The Harrad Experiment*. Los Angeles, CA: Sherbourne Press.

Roscoe, B., Cavanaugh, L.E., & Kennedy, D.R. (1988). Dating infidelity: Behaviors, reasons, and consequences. *Adolescence*, 23, 35–43.

Russell, Bertrand. (1933). *On Education, Especially in Early Childhood*. London, UK: Allen & Unwin.

Scheinkman, M. (2005). Beyond the trauma of betrayal: Reconsidering affairs in couples therapy. *Family Process*, 44, 227–244.

Schmitt, D.P. (2004). The Big Five related to risky sexual behaviour across 10 world regions: Differential personality associations of sexual promiscuity and relationship infidelity. *European Journal of Personality*, 18, 301–319.

Shackelford, D., Buss, M., & Bennet, K. (2002). Forgiveness or breakup: Sex differences in responses to a partner's infidelity. *Cognition and Emotion*, 6(2), 8.

Spanier, G.B., & Margolis, R.L. (1983). Marital separation and extramarital sexual behavior. *Journal of Sex Research*, 19, 23–48.

Spotnitz, Hyman, & Freeman, Lucy. (1964). *The Wandering Husband*. Englewood Cliffs, NJ: Prentice Hall.

Stone, Abraham. (1954, May). The case against marital infidelity. *Readers Digest*, 11–14.

Sweeney, M.M., & Horwitz, A.V. (2001). Infidelity, initiation, and the emotional climate of divorce: Are there implications for mental health? *Journal of Health and Social Behavior*, 42, 295–309.

Treas, J., & Giesen, D. (2000). Sexual infidelity among married and cohabiting Americans. *Journal of Marriage and the Family*, 62, 48–60.

Walker, T., & Ehrenberg, M. (1998). An exploratory study of young person's attachment style and perceived reasons for parental divorce. *Journal of Adolescent Research*, 13, 320–342.

Wardle, Lynn D. (2003, Fall). Parental infidelity and the "no-harm" rule in custody litigation. *Catholic University Law Review*, 52(1), 127.

Watzlawick, Paul, Weakland, John, & Fisch, Richard. (1974). *Change*. New York: Norton.

Weeks, Gerald, & Treat, Stephen (2001). *Couples in Treatment*. New York: Routledge.

Weis, D.L., & Jurich, J. (1985). Size of community of residence as a predictor of attitudes toward extramarital sexual relations. *Journal of Marriage and the Family*, 47, 173–178.

Whisman, M.A., & Snyder, D.K. (2007). Sexual infidelity in a national sample of American women: Differences in prevalence and correlates as a function of method of assessment. *Journal of Family Psychology*, 12, 147–154.

Whitehurst, Robert N. (1969). Extramarital sex: Alienation or extension of normal behavior? In *Extramarital Relations*, edited by G. Neubeck, 129–145. Englewood Cliffs, NJ: Prentice Hall.

Whittey, M.T., & Quigley, L. (2008). Emotional and sexual infidelity offline and in cyberspace. *Journal of Marital and Family Therapy*, 34(4), 461–468.

Winek, Jon L., & Craven, P.A. (2003). Healing rituals for couples recovering from adultery. *Contemporary Family Therapy: An International Journal*, 25(3), 249–266.

Winn, Harold. (1970). Should a husband or wife confess infidelity? *Medical Aspects of Human Sexuality*, 5, 8.

Worthington, E.L. (1998, June). An empathy-humility-commitment model of forgiveness applied within family dyads. *Journal of Family Therapy*, 20, 59–76.

INDEX

About the Author

JOEL BLOCK, PHD, ABPP, is an award-winning psychologist—for excellence in couple therapy—practicing couple and sex therapy in Long Island, New York. Board Certified in couple therapy by the American Board of Professional Psychology (ABPP), Dr. Block is a senior psychologist on the staff of the Northwell Health System and assistant clinical professor (psychology/psychiatry) at the Zucker School of Medicine at Hofstra/Northwell. Block is a fellow of the American Psychological Association (Couple and Family Psychology) and for twenty years he was the doctoral intern training supervisor of the Sexuality Center at the Northwell Health System. Block is the author of more than twenty books on love and sex, his specialty.

About the Sex, Love, and Psychology Series Editor

JUDY KURIANSKY, PHD, is a licensed clinical psychologist and adjunct faculty in the Department of Clinical Psychology at Columbia University Teachers College and the Department of Psychiatry at Columbia University College of Physicians and Surgeons, as well as a visiting professor at Peking University Health Sciences Center and honorary professor in the Department of Psychiatry of the University of Hong Kong. A diplomate of the American Board of Sexology, and fellow of the American Academy of Clinical Sexology, she was awarded the AACS Medal of Sexology for Lifetime Achievement. Kuriansky is a pioneer of sex diagnosis, dating back to being on the DSM III committee; sex therapy evaluation, including early Masters and Johnson therapy; and call-in advice about sex on the radio and TV. A cofounder of the Society for Sex Therapy and Research, and past board member of the American Association of Sex Educators, Counselors and Therapists (AASECT), she has authored hundreds of articles in professional journals, including the *Journal of Marital and Sex Therapy* and SIECUS reports, and mass market articles including those for *Cosmopolitan* and *Family Circle* magazines. She has written sex advice columns worldwide, including for the *South China Morning Post*, *Singapore Straits Times*, *Sankei Sinbun* newspaper, and the *New York Daily News*. She has developed and led hundreds of workshops about sexuality around the world from China and Japan to India, Israel, Iran, Austria and Argentina, including on an integration of Eastern and Western techniques for safe sex and for relationship enhancement.